Pussy Whip: Proven, Powerful "Secret" Technique Controls Your Man

Lanie Stevens

http://laniestevensauthor.com

Disclaimer: This book is offered for personal growth and is not represented as medical, mental, sexual or psychological advice or counseling. Copyright effective 2013. Material is not to be distributed, reproduced, copied or transmitted in any form whatsoever without signed permission and approval by the author.

Table of Contents

Chapter 1 – Unique Technique

*"The question isn't who's going to let me.
It's who is going to stop me?"* – *Ayn Rand*

You don't need to read a book that's 200 pages long that you have to memorize to control or keep your man. You don't need to dress in sexy lingerie, be a femme fatale or force yourself to love and participate in shooting pool or hunting wild animals to win or keep his affection. You don't need to change *who* and *what* you are to attract a man, keep a man or get him to change.

All you need is this instructional guide with my *secret technique* to have him eating out of the palm of your hand any time you desire. Unlike most *self-help* books that give you a laundry list of ways *you* can change to attract or keep a man this book will give you a technique that is simple, fast and powerful.

It's not a *flirting* technique or a kinky *sexual* position – it's an amazing technique that will literally allow you to control your man's thoughts and feelings. Does this sound too good to be true? I assure you that there's no way you can understand just how powerful this technique is until you try it and then you'll be amazed at how fast it works. It's truly magic!

This book is especially powerful if you feel that you're unable to control your man's behavior, thoughts or emotions. If your man has cheated on you, left you for another woman, or is a scoundrel that you're unable to control, this book is for you. Hey, even if he's a sweetheart but you need a little more cooperation, financial freedom, sex, love, admiration or adoration – just read the book. This book will change your life and the way your guy behaves, either around you or with you nowhere near him.

If you're sitting around wondering what to do about your relationship, devising a plan to get your guy back into your arms, are with a control freak and are frustrated, or a cheater you can't control, a cheap ass who refuses to give you what you need, a man who won't commit to you – whatever relationship you're currently in – you are about to experience a drastic positive change in your man's behavior.

All you need to do is use a simple technique for a few minutes each day and he will be your love slave. For faster results, and to supercharge my *secret technique*, a companion meditation is available only on my website. **BUT READ THE BOOK FIRST!**

I've had women (and some sneaky men) use this technique to get their cheating mate back on track, to get him (or her) to do things they'd refused to do, to love them, to adore them, to do things for them, to buy them things or to be under their spell where their every wish was granted. I can literally go on and on, but you have to try this technique yourself.

If this technique sounds magical it's because it is but until now you've probably never heard of something so powerful. The good news is you don't have to believe in magic to try it and have it work! It works, and when you see the proof you'll be a believer! In fact, it can't fail if you follow my simple instructions. Is it worth spending a few minutes of your day to get your man to do what you want, when you want?

Let's use an example of your boyfriend taking off with another woman because it's truly heartbreaking. You've been sitting around secretly wishing he and his new girlfriend would drive off a cliff together, but it isn't working. Neither is visualizing him cheating on her with someone else or her running off with some other woman's mate. Obviously, they're still alive so wishing them a slow, painful death hasn't been productive. (I'm just joking here so please no nasty emails.)

The only thing you've been able to do since he left you is to dream about the jerk and envision how happy the two *lovebirds* are, making your misery even worse if possible. Trust me ladies, when you read this book you'll understand how envisioning their happiness is the **ABSOLUTE WORST** thing you can do.

You need to do something positive. You need to do something that will get him back in your arms and into your bed. You need to stop feeling sorry for yourself and get off your butt. And, you need to do it now! There's hope for you and your relationship. That's the good news! It's time to take back your power and I'm here to help you do it!

If you follow my simple, easy instructions later in this book you'll have him begging you back. Yes, it seems impossible right now but with a proven technique like this one what do you have to lose? This technique allows you to connect with him whenever you desire just using the power of your mind. It is the most powerful weapon you have at your disposal and you can easily influence others when you learn to apply my secret. No harassing him with text messages, phone calls, stalking or emails. Trust me, you'll see how easy it is to get results!

The good news is that not only can you control his thoughts but they will seem like they're his idea and not yours. For instance, you want him to do something for you and he's resisted. You can argue, fight, pout or even breakup over silly and simple things. Or, you can just sit down and close your eyes to connect to your mate and influence them to do exactly what you wanted and have them think you had nothing to do with it. Yeah, maybe it is magic!

You can enhance your current relationship, attract a new guy, make someone you desire think of you instantly and have guys chasing you if that's what you desire. It's really that powerful. Plus, it's very simple to learn and fun to use. It puts the power back into your hands and you'll never let it go again.

Once you begin using this *secret technique* you'll find that you can manifest anything and everything you desire in life. Even your personal life, business life, self-esteem and friendships will all improve. It doesn't take long to manifest positive things in your life when you follow my simple steps.

When will it work? I know people where it's worked like magic instantly or within a couple of days, it depends entirely on *you*. I myself have experienced it working *immediately* and I know *many* others that have experienced fast results, too. The important thing is that **IT WORKS**!

Your man will be unable to stop thinking about you when you use my technique on him.

If you've decided that you want your man to jump through hoops to please you then you need this book. If you want him to love you and only you then I suggest you read this book. I view this book as sharing a secret with my closest and dearest girlfriends. I'm sharing a secret with you that can change your life and your relationship.

It doesn't just work if he left you for another woman, if he's a jerk, a flirt, a player, a grump, a lazy ass or a tightwad. It is the quintessential guide for **ALL WOMEN** who want their men to do what they want them to do. Even if you're currently in a wonderful, fabulous and once-in-a-lifetime relationship this book will only make it *better*. And it works on everyone else in your life, too!

TRUE STORY: A few years ago a Hollywood actress contacted me after reading this book because she wanted her boyfriend back. Her boyfriend worked with her on a popular primetime series and had fallen for an "extra" working with them. She bought my book because she overheard this woman talking to someone about how she'd attracted the boyfriend using the "secret technique" I teach in this book. With my assistance she won her guy back easily but, just as importantly, she supercharged her career because she learned how to influence others in a unique and powerful manner. She stated to me; "I don't know what will happen with my guy but by using your technique HBO has given me the opportunity to star in ANY series of my choosing and they said I didn't even have to do a casting call. My life has never been better!"

Use it for LOVE but also use it for LIFE! ;-)

The title of the book should have been "How To Get ANYONE To Do What You Want Them To Do And Not Realize The Reason" -- but my title was catchier.

I'm going to explain to you specifically how and why my *secret technique* works and then you can practice it until it works perfectly – **FOR YOU**. I'm not talking about taking hours out of your day to master some difficult maneuver. I'm going to give you explicit directions that will change your life and you can follow them quickly, effortlessly, easily, anywhere and any time.

You can use it on anyone you come into contact with during the day not just your boyfriend, lover, husband or *"ex"*. You'll find yourself using the technique every day for many different things that positively affect your life. Why wouldn't you continue to spend a few minutes each day directing and creating your life when you see how effective this secret is? Yes, this technique is truly amazing and life altering! While it isn't using *only* the Law of Attraction it does have facets of it and we're attracting things 24/7 so why not use it to your advantage?

I can't take full credit for the *secret technique* because it was used many, many years ago and pretty effectively. I just read about it, studied it, perfected it, employed it and know beyond a shadow of a doubt that it works. To test the *secret technique* I've taught many friends, clients and acquaintances of both sexes to use it and they have reported back the results to me.

This is **NOT** a typical relationship advice book. It's also **NOT** *specifically* a Law of Attraction book, although it has aspects of both in it. It's a once-in-a-lifetime opportunity to learn a *secret technique* never shared before in an easy to follow step-by-step manner.

You don't have to have a Ph.D. to do the technique properly. Although the title is Pussy Whip there aren't any *pussy exercises* to teach you how to clamp down on his penis until he does what you want in self-defense. It doesn't require hours and hours of practice to work effectively. You don't have to be in the perfect mental health or physical state to have it work.

It works on anyone you want to connect with and influence in your life. Whether it's the person you lost, the person you have, or the person you desire and don't yet have. Whether you're dealing with friends, family, acquaintances, strangers, mates, children, people you love or people you hate – you will be able to influence their thoughts and behavior. Anyone you choose to focus on can be easily persuaded to change, do what you want them to do and feel the emotions you want them to feel AND they'll think it was all their idea!

"Anyone can master it and the results are amazing!"

As a teacher of the Law of Attraction I didn't purposefully seek out a method to control someone else's thoughts, actions or emotions but when I accidentally ran across this amazing technique it literally changed my life. It makes the Law of Attraction seem weak and inadequate by itself but combined with the technique I'm teaching it will magnify results by a thousand percent.

Although I write books on relationships, and have read thousands of relationship books, this technique is very different and unique. This is not a relationship book and it's not going to give you advice on how you can make your relationship better or different in a *typical* manner. The direction and guidance in this book is non-traditional but it's guaranteed to change your thinking. And, it will set you on a quick course to creating the relationship of your dreams.

Most relationship books have something in common. They teach you how to change, play head games, flirt in an attempt to get him to be attracted to you, be a sexpot, or wait two months to have sex, use your sexual appeal or abstain from sex altogether – in other words a lot of advice but little actual steps to success. I'll bet that most of you can't remember a thing from the many books you've read. You read it and forget it. The books, and notes from the books, are stashed in a drawer someplace doing you absolutely no good.

Even if the tips are kick-ass you won't remember them. How can you remember a laundry list of changes you have to make when life is so busy it's hard to remember to pick up milk at the market? Most books give you the same tired techniques, written in different ways, to get or keep your man. In order to do that you have to be around your guy and be better at game playing than he is. While other books may offer great advice, and I'm not knocking their suggested guidance, why would you want to make your life even harder?

Why go through all of the silly mind games when all you need to do is one simple thing?

What if you aren't around your man to influence him? What if you want instant results? What if the A-hole has left you and you don't have interaction to win him back? What if you've already broken the suggested rules that the books recommend? The good news is that it's never too late!

Truly ladies, this book will have any man eating out of the palm of your hand without you doing anything at all but one simple technique. Use this book as an addition to the other great books about relationships. You don't have to only rely on the information in my books, but I know once you learn them you'll never stop using my techniques. He'll be like a puppet on a string that you're influencing and he will love every minute of it. Go ahead, get him *pussy whipped* without lifting a finger!

While it's possible to skip to the part where I explain my technique, I don't advise doing it. Read the entire book so you can understand some basics that are necessary for your success. Read stories of success and know more about the technique than just the steps involved. I hope you enjoy the book because I absolutely love to empower my *sisters*!

TRUE STORY: _A client told me about wanting to meet a specific rock 'n roll superstar and she was going to try the technique on him. I thought, okay but he's being chased by literally hundreds of thousands of fans so what are the chances? I didn't want to discourage her but I thought chances were very slim. She went to his concert and he had one of his roadies ask her to come backstage. The minute he met her it was like he'd known her from a previous meeting. In fact, he asked her "do I know you"? Of course they'd never met but the attraction was instant because she'd used the technique on him many times. He felt the connection and she was treated like a princess at the concert. Since then she's been to several other concerts, she's really a super fan, and each time he seeks her out. The technique makes you connected on a level you haven't experienced before._

Chapter 2 – Influencing Reality

"The meeting of two personalities is like the contact of two chemical substances: if there is any reaction, both are transformed." – *Carl Jung*

The power of your mind is incredible and it's amazing how little we exercise it and use it. We go on autopilot and allow thoughts and feelings to enter that we don't want, don't need and don't desire. With approximately 60,000 thoughts a day it's easy to get distracted by them and most people are unable to control the randomness of thoughts. This book will guide you to using *directed* and *intentional* thoughts to affect and influence *anyone* you choose easily and effortlessly.

Edgar Cayce emphasized almost a century ago the fact that thoughts are *things*. Powerful *things*. Earlier in the book I mentioned that the absolute worst thing you should do is to visualize the jerk *"ex"* that left you and his new girlfriend living a wonderful life together.

Maybe you thought it was because it caused too much pain for you to visualize them but it's much more than that. Believe it or not your positive thoughts about them will make their relationship even stronger. Yes, it will influence whatever bond they have together and your visualization will create their reality. Not exactly what you want to have happen, is it?

Not only will it make their relationship stronger, and more likely to succeed, but the more positive emotion you put into your visualization the happier they'll be. You'll actually be creating and reinforcing their *happy* relationship using the power of your thoughts and emotions. That really sucks doesn't it? I'll let you in on a secret. You can also do the opposite and break up their relationship, too. Learn to use your mind and the benefits are unlimited.

I've always been fascinated with the power of the mind and its' ability to attract based on the Law of Attraction. Focus on a certain thing or outcome, combine it with the feeling you already possess what you desire and voila – it's magically yours. It sounds great but very few people use their thoughts with the focus and emotions required to easily attract what they desire. *Thoughts are things* projected out into the universe landing haphazardly for the most part unless they have direction and purpose.

We are all united on earth, whether we acknowledge it or not, so we're influenced to a degree without having to think much about it. For instance, ever feel someone across a crowded room was looking at you? Ever know that someone was talking about you even if they weren't looking in your direction? Ever think of someone and then your phone rings? Ever have someone cross your mind only to find out they were thinking or talking about you at that exact moment? Ever know what someone was thinking or feeling without him or her saying a word?

You'll answer *yes* to most of the questions because it happens to everyone. Thoughts are things and, even when thoughts aren't directed, you can sometimes pick up on them intuitively. Why is that? The reason is because when you are thinking of someone, or they are thinking about you, it is actually *felt* by the other person because of what quantum physics refers to as *"entanglement"*.

Depending on the strength of their thought you may suddenly wonder if something's wrong with them or you may feel a need to contact them. The reason is because they have *accidentally*, and *unintentionally*, connected to you through entanglement. Being entangled is a power much like the current of electricity. It's something we don't think about or tap into unless needed, it's always ready to be switched on but waiting for the operator to flip the switch.

Entanglement is always there but seldomly used because the operator is asleep or doesn't know where the switch is located. So thoughts are not telepathically delivered to the recipient of your choosing. All you have to do is learn how to turn the power on and flip the switch to deliberately send out any message or emotion you choose.

Imagine what would happen if you had the knowledge of how to direct your thoughts intentionally. You don't have to be a witch or a wizard to influence someone else (your husband, boyfriend, lover, ex, boss, children or a stranger) and affect their behavior or strengthen their connection to you. All you have to do is follow my simple technique and you'll be a success within minutes. *You have the ability right now at this very moment.* You just don't know you have it!

For those of you shaking your heads in disbelief please open your mind. What I'm saying is 100% true! You do realize that you can physically feel the *good* or *bad* thoughts about you and they can manifest themselves in different ways, right? Imagine how someone *feels* when they're prayed over compared to what they may feel when someone's backstabbing them.

If you've ever had an enemy, or had an argument with someone that wasn't resolved, you've most likely experienced the negative thoughts they've sent your way. They can affect your life in ways like clumsiness, illness, bad luck, depression, loss or any number of ways. It's like a curse was placed on you and you probably have no idea what the hell is going on.

The thoughts that are directed at you can and do directly affect your well-being. The only reason they may not affect your behavior is because the person sending the thoughts doesn't know the *secret* to influencing you. They don't have the ability to use their thoughts and direct them using specific steps that create a desired outcome.

Thoughts are real things and the results of thoughts can be truly impressive. They can affect you either positively or negatively but trust me when I say that they can and do affect you. When you learn to direct thoughts to someone it will actually feel as if they themselves are having the thoughts. It doesn't feel to them that's it coming from outside themselves. Your thoughts and feelings will be their thoughts and feelings.

Thoughts are powerful. When I was learning to snow ski the instructor told me not to look in the direction I didn't want to go. Just by directing my attention someplace else it had the potential to send me over a cliff. It's sort of like that with your thoughts. If you don't want something in your life you have to stop thinking about it, focusing on it and getting your emotions involved in the creation of it. Direct your attention away from the thing that you don't want in your life and focus *only* on what you desire.

In the case of an estranged husband or boyfriend it's hard not to be emotional about your loss but you have to re-direct your thoughts. In the case of your current boyfriend, husband or lover, just use the power of your directed thoughts to influence what they're doing and thinking. You can make them think of you in the blink of an eye and whatever you want them to think about you they will think it.

You can't keep visualizing the past and expect things to change. You can't focus on things or behavior that you don't like and expect the future to change. Remember Albert Einstein's definition of insanity:

"Doing the same thing over and over again and expecting a different result".

If you want to change the future with your man you have to change your belief. Changing the way you think will change the way you feel and changing the way you feel will bring about positive results in your life. Thoughts affect your life whether you're using the Law of Attraction or the techniques I teach you. *Thoughts are powerful!*

During the 1990's, Dr. Masaru Emoto performed a series of experiments observing the physical effects of words, thoughts, prayers, music and environment on the crystalline structure of water. He hired photographers to take pictures of water after it was exposed to variables and subsequently frozen so that they would form crystalline structures. The results were nothing short of remarkable.

If you haven't read his book, or seen the pictures he's taken of water, please check out his book <u>The Hidden Messages in Water</u>. It's one of the most fascinating studies on thoughts I have ever read.

The photographers took photos of water that was polluted and contaminated before and after prayer. Before prayer the water was muddy, nasty and *looked* like it was polluted. After prayer the droplets resembled snowflakes and each one was different, yet perfect. Thoughts are things and they can – and do – change the very essence of our being.

Our bodies are comprised of at least 60-70% water so what do you think thoughts do to our bodies? Thinking that we are fat, old, ugly, useless, unloved, unwanted, inferior or other negative thoughts will morph us into a *polluted lake*. Focusing on negative things that we don't want in our lives will cause them to manifest. Focusing on creation, love, attachment, and happiness and togetherness with your mate cause them to manifest.

Believing that you're special, unique, cared for, blessed, gifted, smart and beautiful will make the water in your body special and holy. You will literally become what you believe you are. It's a universal law. Believe that you have the ability to do anything you choose, be anyone you choose and have anyone you choose – because you do!

Edgar Cayce was a fascinating man with gifts that haven't been duplicated by anyone else. Using just the power of his mind he would allow himself to go into a trance-like state while a scribe took dictation about his experiences. He could literally transport his energetic aura into the room of the person he was *reading* wherever they were in the world. His thoughts and beliefs created an amazing reality. I suggest if you haven't read any of his books that you go online and get a few on different subjects.

Edgar Cayce was able to tell what the person he was reading was wearing, what they were doing, diagnose their medical problems and give them a prescription to cure them all while he was in a meditative state. The power of the subconscious mind is powerful and if you learn to CONTROL and DIRECT it through intention there is nothing that cannot be accomplished.

Sure, this sounds *woo-woo* to those of you who've never studied anything like it. I assure you after reading all of his books and manuscripts that this man was a phenomenon that hasn't been duplicated. He could go into such detail in his prescriptions that he would tell the patient exactly which shelf the ingredients were located on, at a pharmacy thousands of miles from where he was living. Are you impressed yet?

I remember when I read his *thoughts are things* statement and how emphatic he was that you never, ever think or dwell on something that you don't want to have happen to you. I'm sure you think logically that it makes sense because just thinking about something bad may cause it to happen. That's logical, right?

Well, it's more logical than we even know. Just thinking about something draws it to us because we are creating it. We are visualizing it, living it, experiencing it in our minds and causing it to happen in our lives. It didn't happen to us – it happened because of us. While this is the Law of Attraction in action the technique I'll teach you requires you to visualize, live and experience emotions and direct your thoughts.

If our thoughts are directed at something that we can see, feel and experience in our minds we become a magnet for it to manifest. How can it fail?

Okay, so now you're thinking about all the things that you don't want to happen and how they happen anyway, right? I have a friend who'll argue with me over the fact that she's a positive person but all these bad things happen to her anyway. Now I can't get into her head and know what she's thinking, but if her conversations are any indication then her thoughts will go kind of like this:

"I can see that couple over there and I want what they have. I want to have a relationship like theirs instead of one like mine. Why can't I ever have a good relationship? Why do I always end up with the sorry jerks? What's wrong with me? Why is it that nobody loves me? I hate myself because I'm unlovable. That's it, I will never find someone to love me like that couple over there. Oh yes, Lanie said I need to think positive thoughts. So, let's see – I wish I had someone to love me. I really want someone to care for me!"

You won't be surprised that she's so negative that she unknowingly projects her thoughts to her mate and they have an extremely unhappy relationship. I've explained that she's entangled with him so he feels her thoughts, whether he's aware or not, and they are negatively affecting their relationship. If you imagine your thoughts to be that bubble over someone's heads in old cartoons you would be right. Thoughts are real and they hang around in space and time affecting those the thoughts are about as well as innocent bystanders.

The vibration of thoughts affect the entire planet and you can certainly feel them if you pay attention to the energy of places you go. I don't like going to Vegas because the energy is one of desperation, vulgarity, drunkenness and chaos. To me it's a disturbing energy and I can only take 2-3 days of it before I have to leave. Some people resonate with it and can even block the negativity of the energy to always win money.

I know a woman who always wins when she plays slot machines. Even at the airport she'll win and the odds there are the worst of all the gambling places in Vegas. The reason she always wins is because she expects to win and never *thinks* about losing. It never enters her mind that she may not win! She doesn't check out the machines, look at how much money the person lost before her, put her hands in front to feel the energy – she just walks over and puts her money in and I swear she wins almost every time.

There's a man who has won a multi-million dollar lottery drawing TWICE.

What are the odds of that happening? When interviewed he said he wasn't surprised in the least. These people have the belief and attitude of winners and their positive thoughts influenced their reality. The man who won the lottery said he expected to win the second time. Unbelievable? Yes, but absolutely true. Winners believe and know how to project their thoughts to attract what they desire. It's really as simple as that.

So, if thoughts are things what will you do with your thoughts? Will you sit around and visualize the ex-boyfriend being happy without you? Or, will you visualize him being happy **ONLY** with you? Will you focus on what you don't like about your current man? Or, will you focus on what you want him to be like and change him to be better suited to you? Will you project positive thoughts to others or will you influence them using negativity?

By the end of this book you'll have the power to influence anyone you choose by directing your thoughts in a specific manner. How will you use your knowledge? Will you change your relationship? Create a new opportunity? Attract a truck load of money? The power to influence another person is something most of us dream about but never accomplish. The time is now to change it, *girlfriends*!

TRUE STORY: I've only had **one** crush on a celebrity in my life and the likelihood of me meeting him was slim to none. I mean how in the world would I meet someone who lived in California when I live in Texas? One day I was having lunch with a girlfriend and she brought along one of her female friends. As we were talking about different subjects she mentioned that she'd met a well-known celebrity at a party recently. When she said his name I'm sure I looked shocked but I never said anything about me crushing on him for years. As she was telling us the story of how they met, what he was like in person and other details I was busy using my technique on her. I mentally sent her the message; *"If there is ever another party you'll invite me to it"*. About 6-8 months later I got a phone call from my girlfriend saying that her friend had been invited to a party that she expected my secret crush to attend. She said; *"Why don't you invite Lanie because I feel she'd enjoy meeting him?"* I went to the party and he was there. Unbelievably he spent the entire evening talking to me to the exclusion of everyone else except to take a few photos. We dated until I went back to the man I'd been in love with for years. Expect the unexpected!

Some would say this was just a coincidence but I know of the over 300 million people in the United States the person I'd be least likely to meet is my one and only *crush*. Plus, I didn't really know the person who invited me to the party and never saw her again. When I reached out and touched her mind with my thoughts she responded. It's as simple as that. .

What you're actually doing when using the technique going through the steps or standing in front of someone is meeting them halfway. When you call out to them they unknowingly respond to you. Sort of like when you hear someone say your name and you are in the middle of a loud crowd of people. Your ears will perk up without seeing or being able to fully hear what the person is saying. Thoughts are tangible things.

Chapter 3 – Influencing Thoughts

Edgar Cayce taught the power of your thoughts but there was another mentor who opened up the world of influencing others with the power of your thoughts. His name was Neville Goddard and he was the forefather of books like <u>The Law of Attraction</u> by Esther Hicks. He wrote exclusively about the Law of Attraction and it was his book that shared how you could do *one specific thing* and it would immediately influence another person. His books are difficult to read, and even understand because of the way they're written, but they're so powerful they blow everyone else's away.

Don't get me wrong <u>The Law of Attraction</u> is a wonderful book but, in my opinion, it is mainly a *feel-good* book. It does open your eyes to the fact that magical things can and will happen if you follow some basic principles. It doesn't teach you the steps to influence someone else's mind and behavior and that's what my technique teaches you. Although I discovered the original technique from reading Neville's books I've tweaked it to be even more mind blowing and amazing.

The Law of Attraction teaches you can visualize, and live as if you have already achieved success, and hope to attract something positive in your life. That's a great way to live your life in general. If you are kind and loving surely you'll attract a mate who is, too. That's just a good philosophy in life. In reality if you follow your passion in life, using your emotions as the fuel for your desire, you'll attract all kinds of wonderful things.

If you believe in the Law of Karma you may do things because you don't want some bad crap coming back to you so the reason may be questionable but the deeds are positive. I know someone who tithes at church only because they feel they're buying good karma. Sometimes it doesn't matter if the person is only being generous so they have good things returned to them. If it works for them it's fine!

Neville Goddard lived his life as a genuine religious and spiritual person and he had *really* great karma. Plus, he's positively affected several generations of people seeking answers and guidance in life. And, he did something that was special and unique to him and he shared it in *one* book that changed my entire life.

Neville shared the *secret* to influencing someone else's thoughts and actions and made it so simple very few people understood the method or the power of the guidance. *In fact, it was almost too simple.* And, it was written about in only one paragraph in all of his books!

People believe the harder something is the better and that's just not the case.

I've never counted how many books Neville published but it was at least a dozen or more. All of his books addressed pretty much the same subject but they just basically said the same thing in different ways. I think he was hoping that his audience would hear the different ways he wrote the message and resonate to one or more of them.

That's the reason a lot of books, maybe mine included; seem to say some of the same things a little differently. Readers will resonate with some things, and not with others, so it's a way to reach them on different levels.

I've read literally all of his books but only a few of them had a message that I heard loud and clear. His message on mind control was so powerful and unique that he wrote about it only *once* in all of his books and he never wrote about it again. I think he realized that people could use it for either positive or negative things and he didn't want to be responsible. I believe that it was so effective that the knowledge and power of the technique scared him a little.

I loved all of his books but there was a message in one book that made me feel like I was thunderstruck. I mean my body and mind literally *felt* the power of this one passage that changed my life. Amazingly, it was one of the shortest passages in the book and he never repeated it again that I could find. But it was a message that I practiced until I became a master. It was so easy to do I was amazed.

In this one paragraph I read a technique that was so simple, so powerful, and impactful that it literally changed my life forever.

In fact, I'll never forget the first time I used the technique. The results were so impressive and immediate that I almost fell out of bed laughing. *How the hell can something so easy and simple be so effective?* My mind was blown wide open with the power I'd just received from my mentor.

My readers have asked for the exact passage in his book that changed my life and I haven't gone back over the thousands of pages necessary to find it. One of the most powerful passages I've ever read and I can't locate it.

It doesn't matter because I have it memorized, and have practiced it thousands of times, over a period of many years. Not only have I practiced it but I've also perfected it. If there were only one thing I could take with me from this life I have to tell you that the power of manifesting, and positively influencing others, using only my thoughts would be the *one thing.*

Before I even tell you how to do the visualization, and the technique, I want to share my very first experience with you. If I don't tell you about the very first time I tried it, and the results I achieved, then you may not even read enough of this book to find out how to do it yourself.

I was lying in bed next to my boyfriend reading Neville's book and it was past midnight. My ex-boyfriend John and I were seeing each other at the time and things weren't going well between us. We were arguing before we went to bed and we were barely speaking. I don't even know why I was spending the night with him because I should have just gone home rather than stay with him and be miserable.

But believing in universal guidance I now know and understand clearly the reason I stayed at John's home that night. It allowed me to practice the hidden nugget I was about to discover in Neville's book. The technique that would change my life!

If I'd been alone then I wouldn't have gotten the instant gratification of seeing it work within seconds. It would've still worked but I may not have realized it until John mentioned it to me and that's probably something he wouldn't have done. So I wouldn't have known that it worked so fast *or* that it worked at all. Without confirmation I probably wouldn't have continued to practice it. This was not a coincidence.

I had just finished reading the passage in the book that described how to "*get him to do and say what*

I wanted him to". There are some books that give you a general idea of the concept of *mind over matter* but this book gave me the steps involved.

To my utter and complete amazement it actually worked instantly! This is more than mind over matter. This is the power of creating what you desire! I will remember that moment for the rest of my life!

Let me explain that John had a mind that was slammed totally closed and just getting into his brain should've been a huge feat. So I wouldn't have believed for a second that anything I did that was *woo-woo,* or out there, would ever work on Mr. Non-Religious, Non-Spiritual, Agnostic, Non-Believing Man.

Not that you have to believe in anything at all spiritually or religiously to have this technique work. In fact, I'm sure you can be an atheist and still have it work for you. This technique is not a prayer it's using the power of your thoughts and *entanglement.* Although when Neville wrote the book there wasn't terminology that explained the phenomenon. He just knew it worked!

After I read the instructions for the technique I laid the book on my stomach to do exactly what the instructions said to do. I didn't have expectations, although I understood the power of the passage immediately upon reading it. I didn't feel nervous, anxious or fearful that it would or wouldn't work as many of my readers have expressed they felt. I was just sort of playing around and had no pre-conceived notions. Which I learned later was the *exact frame of mind* to be in to manifest results.

Now I understand how having feelings of expectation can cause the technique to be less effective because if you don't believe in something you try it in a half-assed manner. At the time I was just having fun and toying with the idea of something so simple being so powerful. The total time of my focus and attention to John took all of about 5 minutes maximum the first time.

I didn't feel anything, see anything or hear any voices speaking to me. It was just a simple, easy-to-do exercise and I didn't expect huge results. I certainly didn't expect what happened next!

Before I could even pick up my book to continue reading John sat straight up in bed. *I had just been using the technique on him using the instructions I learned only a few minutes before!* I was so shocked at first that I didn't think it had anything to do with what I'd been doing mentally to him.

I thought maybe he was ill because just a few minutes earlier he looked like he was in a dead sleep. Or, he could have been playing possum because he was so pissed at me he didn't want any interaction. Regardless, he had his back turned to me and appeared to be totally disconnected and knocked out.

Suddenly he sat straight up in bed and said *precisely* what I wanted to hear him say! He repeated, in his own words, what I had visualized him saying during my brief 5-minute exercise. What I wanted him to do for me, that he'd been resisting, was agreed upon within minutes of using this technique. And, it wasn't a little thing! It was a huge concession on his part! I almost burst out laughing because after he repeated the words to me he said, *"Now I'm going to sleep without any further discussion"*. Holy crap!

This was the neatest trick I've ever seen. Thank you universe for making me spend the night with this grumpy prick because I got to see how fast this *secret technique* works. Remember, there are no coincidences in life. My being there at that moment in time not only helped me but it has also allowed thousands of women to learn about this technique through me and my books.

That night I also focused on two other messages I wanted to send to people that I hadn't heard from in a while. I was going to see if the results with John had been a fluke. I visualized one friend telling me he'd take me to lunch and treat me – he was sort of a cheapskate. I visualized the other one calling to see how I was doing. I focused on people that I hadn't heard from in several months so it would be unlikely they'd contact me out of the blue.

It was a test so I wanted to make it difficult! In this experiment I wanted confirmation that the technique definitely worked and it wasn't just a weird and crazy accident. So I guess I focused on each person

I was sending a message to for about two or three minutes. It's funny that the first time I did it, and got results, was the time that I expected absolutely nothing to happen. Later, after thousands of emails from readers and users of this technique, I understand that the more expectations you have the less power the technique has. And, the more you let go of any pre-conceived ideas the faster you get results.

I get letters from readers who get immediate results and then freeze up on subsequent attempts. The best way to get results is to do the technique, let any expectations go and not worry about the results! Don't block your success by trying to force it, believing that success only shows up in certain ways or not at all, or putting time limitations on getting results. While this is different than regular Law of Attraction you still have to have faith and belief in the process.

The next morning I was still chuckling over John sitting up in bed and telling me what I told him mentally to say when I received two messages from the friends I'd used the technique on the night before. One friend sent me an email and wanted to take me to lunch and said it would be his treat. The other friend left a voicemail saying he felt like he needed to contact me immediately because I popped into his mind so strongly. He was worried that something had happened to me because he couldn't get me off his mind. Pretty powerful stuff!

Now I've had numerous other success stories since the first time I started using this technique *many* years ago. But I wanted you to hear about the very first time I tried it and the success I experienced. I don't have special powers so the good news is that if I can do it – **YOU CAN DO IT**!

I'm not going to guarantee you that it will work that dramatically for you the first time you give it a try. Or, better stated I will say that the technique will always work, whether you get confirmation or not, because you can't fail to connect with whomever you choose to connect to. It works instantly to get your thoughts to your intended target whether they acknowledge them or not. Plus, they'll think the thoughts are their own. And, if you do this technique daily your results may be absolutely amazing. Why do I say that?

IT HAS NEVER FAILED!!!

I have a friend who dated this creep for at least 5 years. He was a total douche and he doesn't deserve the time it takes for me to write about him. I don't know why my friend continued to see him when he offered so little but she did and I respected her choice.

He's married and he saw my friend only when it was convenient for him. Of course, he only saw her when he wanted to get laid. He never told her he loved her, needed her or even cared about her. She decided she wanted to change him. *Right girlfriend, don't we all want to change the pricks we're with I thought to myself?*

After 5 years there wasn't much hope for a change because he certainly didn't think he needed to change and he had proven he was unwilling. He felt like he could continue to do what he wanted, and she'd always be there, because that was their established pattern. It had been 5 years that he had treated her like dirt so what were the odds that he would change unless he chose to?

He had her trained to do what he wanted her to do and he had to do nothing in exchange. What a great deal for him! He had her exactly where he wanted her and no amount of begging, threats or breakups ever fazed the guy. Believe me she tried every trick in the book to coerce him and so far she'd failed miserably.

My friend knew I had a technique that had shown amazing success but she just isn't a believer of anything. I never pushed her to learn the technique and I didn't volunteer to teach it to her. I believe if people want something badly enough they'll seek out the answers. I don't push my thoughts or beliefs on anyone but if they ask I'll share with them because I do like to empower my *sisters*.

Finally, she asked for my help and wanted me to teach her my *secret technique* after five years of struggling with her relationship. I taught her the exact technique I'm going to teach you. The same technique I used on poor, unsuspecting John. We were speaking on the phone when I went through the steps with her explaining in detail so there would be no way for her to not do it precisely. Even though being precise isn't absolutely necessary *she believed it was* so I spent an hour on the phone with her while she took notes.

It's simple to learn but it seemed like it took her forever. She called me over the course of several days making sure that she had all the instructions correct. She kept asking *"are you sure that's all I have to do?"* Yes, I'm positively sure. I told her to *"just do what I am telling you to do"* and you only need to spend a few minutes a day doing it. She wanted instant results so I told her to do it three times a day for a few minutes each time to see what happened. More isn't necessarily better, but I was sick of explaining that to her. Besides spending 10-20 minutes a day isn't too much to ask if you truly want something as badly as she seemed to want it.

She actually used the technique on him for a few days and that totally surprised me. I love her but she's a person who doesn't take control of her life, is a constant victim and can't see that she has the power and ability to change her life. Also, she never sticks to anything for very long and she moves from one thing to another searching for something that works without any effort on her part. So I was kind of impressed that she used the technique for as long as she did. She's someone who calls me constantly, complains each and every time and wonders why her life never changes. Anyway, that's another subject I won't go into now.

After three days she gets a phone call from the *douche bag* (I mean love of her life) telling her that he can't live without her. He loves her. He just has to see her and be with her. He hounded her like crazy until she gave in and saw him. She called me in total and complete shock over the sudden and drastic change in the man she hadn't been able to change for 5 years. I was only surprised because I wasn't sure she had the ability to actually focus on something positive happening in her life.

I wasn't surprised that the technique works because it ALWAYS works!

When she saw the guy he actually had tears in his eyes when telling her how much he loved her. That's right, this cold-hearted jerk was crying because he felt so much emotion for my friend. Is there any doubt that this technique worked like magic on him? He couldn't get enough of her, became somewhat co-dependent and she ended up not wanting him around because she decided she deserved better – but the fact remains that she changed him and he told her what she wanted to hear.

When you witness something totally out of character for a man you've known for that long either:

1) he was struck by a lightning bolt in the middle of the night that caused significant brain damage, or

2) the technique you used on him worked!

He was living proof that the technique will work on anyone regardless of how bad the relationship *is or was*, how long you've been apart or how long you've been together, how well you know the person or even if you don't know them at all. Ladies, it works!

I'm trying to convince you for your own good, not for mine. I know without a doubt that it works like nothing I've ever tried or used. I wouldn't be using a technique for many, many years if it didn't work. There's nothing that works better or faster for manifesting. Period.

If I weren't convinced by my own experiences then I would surely have to be convinced by hers as well as others. Right after I learned the technique I was teaching it to literally everyone I came into contact with who expressed an interest in learning. They would hear my stories and they would be amazed by the results. They would try the experiment and get results, too. I would be amazed by their results.

Over many years of using the technique I'm no longer amazed because I know that anything and everything can and does happen. I just smile when I hear success stories because I've just helped another *sister* which is the total reason I am writing the books in the first place.

In my friend's case there was just one problem. Just as you live your life day-by-day and moment-by-moment you also have to dedicate a few minutes a day to *creating* your awesome life. My friend let up on her married boyfriend and he went back to being a dick. I would remind her to use the technique and sure enough he'd come around again. She'd stop using it and he'd drift away.

I'm not saying that in all cases it's a constant struggle to retain the upper hand and control or to get someone to do what you desire. In many cases there's true love involved and your mate will have an *awakening* where he realizes that he doesn't want to be without you and will do absolutely anything for you. Although initially it may be due to your mental influence it won't remain that way. In my friend's case the guy could really care less and she was controlling him and his feelings, which I don't recommend long term. Why? If there's love involved you don't need to constantly use the technique to put feelings of love in his heart. Also, there's better use of your time and energy than being obsessed with a guy who isn't that into you.

Use it to create a wonderful life with someone but not to constantly manipulate and control his emotions. It's best to ignite the feelings that are already there, place thoughts in his mind when you want something you're not getting and enjoy life together. Don't try to micro-manage and control the poor dude.

"If the guy is not that interested in you it will be difficult to maintain the schedule of controlling him continuously".

The lesson with my friend is that it doesn't matter what you know if you don't practice it. I can teach you something but if you won't take the few minutes it takes a day to be successful you'll find things will gradually go back to the way they were. It takes 30 days to make something a habit. Knowing the technique won't help if you don't practice using it.

You'll do this technique every day for the rest of your life (if you want to use it for more than a mate) so put a note on your headboard. Anything you can do to remember that you're creating your life! If you get your body in awesome condition, because you've worked out like a demon, you aren't going to go stuff yourself with Krispy Kreme donuts or gobs of French fries every day are you?

Well, when you start getting the results from this technique don't start neglecting to do the exercise. When the idiot that left you comes crawling back to you don't forget to continue doing the exercise. Envision keeping him, too. Visualize the home you'll share, the babies you'll chase, the faithfulness he'll give and the great job you desire. In other words, visualize the life of your dreams!

DO NOT SHARE THE SECRET TECHNIQUE WITH A MAN.

This technique is so powerful that we need to keep it for the ladies only. Men have enough power in the world and they don't need something that can control women any more than they already possess. I realized not to share with men when I taught the technique to a previous boyfriend that used it to influence *me*. I suspected it only because I teach the technique and my own emotions and actions were suspicious. He admitted using it and I vowed never to make the mistake again. Unless you're willing to have this technique used against you I suggest you keep it as a secret.

Ladies, when Neville wrote his book with similar information in it he stated emphatically;

"This can make people do things against their will".

I can affirm that it can and does! I've also used it to do a couple of naughty things, too. I'm embarrassed to admit that I used the technique to cause pain to John but at the time I didn't realize the full impact of the power of my knowledge.

He stalked me for two years, said horrible things to me, threatened me, slandered me to friends and absolutely refused to leave me alone. I exploded in a very unique and different way!

TRUE STORY: Using my technique I visualized squeezing John's testicles as hard as I could every day for a week. There was no way to confirm it worked so I didn't give it any more thought. A few months later John and I had to meet up about business and we met over drinks. During the course of our conversation he told me about having an MRI done that day and, although I didn't really care, I asked him what the problem was. He said; *"I'm having this extreme pain in my testicles that drops me to my knees without warning and they can't figure out what's going on. I've had blood work, gone to the urologist and just got the MRI and no answers yet."* I gulped my drink down in two swigs and ordered another one before asking him; *"How long has this been going on, John?"* He told me he'd experienced it for three months. Exactly the amount of time that I'd started the technique on him. I was truly speechless!

I wish I could say that I felt regret but at that time I didn't. He'd feel my wrath again before he finally left me alone.

TRUE STORY: Using my technique I visualized squeezing John's heart as tightly as possible several times. I was at the end of my visualization, and still lying on my bed, when I received a frantic phone call from John. He said; *"I think I'm having a heart attack but it feels weird. It's like something is squeezing my heart and the feeling is so different I probably need to go to the hospital."* I pushed my mute button on the phone before busting a gut laughing. I finally said to him; *"No, I think you'll be fine just lie down for a while"*. Poor John. I almost felt sorry for him but he'd been so vile I couldn't quite fake sympathy.

I admitted to him what I'd done but he refused to believe I could affect his body using only the power of my mind – however he did stop messing with me! The best part of this technique is there is no way to detect that someone's using it, no way to stop it and no way to determine that what you are experiencing isn't coming from within your own body or mind.

The power of emotion combined with the technique can absolutely ruin someone's life. I have a close friend who worked for a man who was one of the wealthiest men in the United States. He fired her because she refused his sexual advances. She destroyed his life using the *secret technique.*

He went from having a huge, successful, thriving business to bankruptcy and jail after a series of other unfortunate events happened to him. You may not believe it, and I totally understand if you don't, but these things began only two weeks after she started using the secret technique on him. This is the series of events as they unfolded:

- He was in a helicopter crash and spent 3 months in the hospital;

- He got out of the hospital only to be overcome with toxic gas in his multi-million dollar home;

- A few months later he was racing his Ferrari and wrecked it which caused another few months in the hospital;

- Over the next couple of years he lost his successful business;

- He was investigated and arrested for child pornography;

- He went to prison for several years;

- He now lives in a trailer in the country!!!!!

No exaggeration in any of this because she's one of my best friends and I witnessed it all. He had a friend contact her after her ex-boss was overcome with the toxic fumes in his home and his request was *"please take the spell off of me!"* He knew it wasn't a coincidence as to the timing and he was paying for all of the past deeds against her and others that he had abused.

My girlfriend was supporting two children without any child support when she was let go from a position of authority with his company. She was evicted from her home and had to ask friends for financial assistance because of the hardship he'd caused. I understand why she sought revenge.

The power of your intentional and directed thoughts can cause things to happen that will knock your socks off. However, I don't recommend using this technique for anything except positive and loving things! I've learned over the years that, while I have the ability to negatively affect someone's life, it's not the highest and best use of the technique.

Sending loving, kind and nurturing thoughts to someone will get you better and more long-lasting results as well as be uplifting for **YOU**. Focus on the positive and you will receive it in return.

TRUE STORY: One of my clients had the most tumultuous relationships I'd ever witnessed between a couple. She wasn't married to the guy but they had been together 4-5 years. She was absolutely head over heels in love and, even though they didn't seem to be a good match, she wasn't about to give him up. They'd broken up more times than I could count and she'd been so distraught she attempted suicide at one point. I advised her to leave him and take back control of her life. She didn't listen to me, and she refused to give him up, although the outcome didn't look good long-term. He wouldn't commit to marriage because of their repeated breakups. She would get upset and leave only to return so they were on a merry-go-round of emotions. Finally, out of sheer desperation, I taught her the technique to see if there was any way they could live peacefully together. She was as excited as a child with a new toy! The next month she told me he'd gotten emotionally closer to her. I was shocked and cautiously optimistic. Within six months he proposed. By the end of that year they were married. They've now started a family and she continues to use the technique and is happier than ever!

I love it when readers or clients share their amazing results. This is especially true when they've been married for a long time, have a family and feel an obligation to not destroy their family unit. We live in an era where simply tossing something away is easier than fixing it. This was truly a *"happy ever after"* ending.

Chapter 4 – How to Influence Your Mate

"Do you believe in telepathy? No! Then what are you doing when you pray?

You may find that this chapter makes it seem *way* too easy to be effective. I assure you that the technique is not only effective it is *very* effective. Not only is it effective but also when you master the technique it'll work very quickly and effortlessly. In the story I told earlier about using the technique the first time on John you can see that the results can take place immediately. It's because it involves connecting consciously by tapping into your subconscious mind.

Your conscious mind is like being the operator of a computer. The subconscious mind is like the software on your computer. You have to be able to use the software if you expect to operate your computer effectively. Our subconscious mind is responsible for approximately 95% of our reality and the conscious mind is estimated to affect the other 5%.

Your subconscious mind is the driving force in your reality. To use it just enter into a meditative or relaxed state of mind. My *secret technique* uses the subconscious mind to affect the behavior of others and it uses it through what quantum physics calls *entanglement.*

What is *entanglement?* You can find out a lot of information on entanglement on-line but the technical definition is:

"Quantum entanglement is a physical phenomenon that occurs when pairs or groups of particles are generated, interact, or share spatial proximity in ways such that the quantum state of each particle cannot be described independently of the state of the others, even when the particles are separated by a large distance."

What does that mean in layman's terms? That you are connected to each and every person you come into contact with and the more intimately you have been involved the greater your connection. How does that benefit you? You can use this entanglement to connect with *any* person anytime you choose. You can influence them, you can send them thoughts, you can heal them at a distance, you can make them desire you, think of you, miss you – *the list goes on and on.* And, they can't stop the interaction from happening and have no idea they're being influenced.

How does that work? Your subconscious mind (the 95% of you that makes up your reality) is the connection to the other person's subconscious mind when using this technique. You may not realize it, but you have an aura surrounding your physical body that goes out several feet or even enough to fill up an entire room. Your energetic body can be projected wherever you choose by directing it through *"thoughts are things"* philosophy.

How do I know that personally? I had an out-of-body experience so I know how small my physical body was in comparison to my etheric body. Also, I know that wherever I wanted to be I was there *instantly* during this experience. The point is that your connection is real! It isn't imagined and, when you're visualizing the way I'm going to teach you, the ability to connect directly with someone is powerful. Think of it like having a secret connection to them that only you have the combination to.

This isn't mumbo-jumbo or junk science. Albert Einstein was the first to discover that entanglement existed and that when two particles, like a pair of electrons are *entangled*, it's impossible to measure one without learning something about the other. They are connected through space and time. It's what Neville Goddard used in his techniques but he didn't know the scientific name for the process. *Entanglement!*

As MIT Physicist David Keiser said: "Somehow what happens to one particle can have an impact on what we would expect the second one to do, even if those particles are nowhere near each other." This is what Einstein termed "spooky action at a distance". The ability for one particle to impact another without being close to one another. You can be lying in bed next to the person or in another country and still affect them.

There was a study done where two people, who didn't know each other, were used as experimentation of this *spooky action at a distance*. They were placed in an underground bunker type enclosure so nothing could interfere and thought transference would be unlikely. They meditated together for a period of time and then they were separated into different rooms with concrete walls between them.

They shone a light in the eyes of one participant while they were connected to a machine that measures brain activity (EEG) and when they did this a certain part of the brain lit up. At the same moment in time the person in the other room's EEG did *exactly* the same thing without a light being shone in their eyes.

It's a fascinating subject but it explains such phenomenon as distance healing, thought transference and how petri dish molecules affect each other. *We are all connected.* The connection is increased and magnified when there's an *intentional* connection.

In the case of the two people meditating, they'd been focusing on each other so the results were easier to measure. How do you connect if the other person isn't aware or willing? *Using the secret technique.*

There's no way for the other person to block the interaction. Just think about John when I used it for physical sensations. He didn't have the ability to block what was happening to him and didn't believe me when I told him how I did it. When I was lying next to him in bed, and using the technique, he sat straight up and told me what I wanted to hear. In his mind they were his thoughts and he had just experienced an "Aha" moment. If he had any way to prevent what happened he would have without a doubt.

I used entanglement when I took back a dress that I shouldn't have been able to return after having it a year with no receipt. I simply sent the message to her mentally, while she was talking, that she'd take the dress back. Not only did she return it but she gave me the money back in cash which I hadn't even requested. My readers have used entanglement to:

- get a marriage proposal;
- improve their marriage;
- get someone to ask them out;
- make their mate desire them again;
- soften their mate;
- change unwanted behavior;
- keep their man faithful;
- and, a myriad of other things.

Sometimes I get asked if it's *too* manipulative. It's no more manipulative than begging, pleading, coercing or any other thing we use to hopefully improve our lives. What happens when you manipulate others? They resent it. They will never know you've influenced them when you use this method!

TRUE STORY: A client had been in a bad marriage for 3-4 years before she left her husband. While she was living with him he treated her horribly. Although she didn't want him back she wanted him to experience what she had felt. Using the technique he suddenly believed that he couldn't live without her and pursued her for more than three years! He begged, pleaded, cried and lost a lot of weight because he was grieving her loss so badly. This was not accidental or unplanned. This is what she visualized during her meditation while using the technique. The man who could care less about her when they lived together was now suffering and believing that he couldn't live without her. This went on for over three years!!! Before the technique he was moving on with his life and dating other women. Afterwards he ONLY wanted her and refused to move on!

She wasn't there personally to inflict the emotional pain on him but he desired her so badly that it almost drove him crazy. Every day, several times a day she would use the technique for no more than ten minutes. He never knew why he so felt so desperate to get her back and he never will. At this point it's been well over five years since she left him and to this day he hasn't moved on with his life or gotten over her loss.

I know you're wondering how it works and why I'm explaining the subconscious and entanglement to you when all you want to do is use the damn technique. You need to understand that it isn't your conscious mind that utilizes the technique. It is the relaxed, subconscious mind that responds to visualization.

The best state to be in is the alpha state. This is the state of mind you experience right before you fall asleep or when you're super relaxed and chill. The alpha state is the manifesting state as well as the state of influencing others. I have meditations on my website that guide you into the alpha state so if you have difficulty please check them out. Yes, you can do it on your own but to guide yourself through meditation is using your conscious mind. That's the mind you're trying to bypass. In the example used of the two people meditating together it was the alpha state that connected them so strongly and effectively.

What's the most opportune time to use the technique? Any time you think about it but certainly in the morning or at night before sleeping! Instead of brooding over the loss of your ex, settling for a broken relationship or marriage, or becoming a victim, just use the simple technique to connect to the person and plant positive thoughts and feelings. You will never feel helpless again.

Have you ever been driving down a street or highway and realized that you are in a trancelike state? It's a moment where you realize that your conscious mind isn't operating and you have been on auto pilot. It may shock you back into reality because you realize (or think) that you could have run off the highway or run over someone due to negligence.

That's the state of mind you want to be in when you practice this technique. You want to be in the state of mind where you have shifted your awareness from your outer world to your inner world. The state where anything is possible and your subconscious mind, the mind that believes anything you tell it to believe, is activated and ready to connect.

Okay ladies, you're ready for your first exercise. Don't use your conscious mind to try to direct your thoughts or feelings during this exercise! It's like exercising too hard or lifting weights that are too heavy and it isn't necessary. Read the steps and then do the exercise after relaxing your body mentally for a few minutes. Don't try to read the steps and do the exercise at the same time. Read and understand the steps and then close your eyes and do it – you get the picture.

It's so simple that it may feel like it's doing nothing. I assure you it is! Remember my first time with John? It works instantly even if you don't get confirmation from your target. Just go to my forum, read my book reviews or talk to someone who's used it and they'll confirm to you that it works.

I am 100% positive that it works and I have many, many people besides myself that have proven it.

You don't have to work hard at anything during this exercise! This exercise requires a *belief that it'll work* and a *shifting of your awareness*. I do this several times during the day and with a variety of people. I don't have to go into an altered state of mind because I have mastered the process of slowing my brain down a little and focusing.

You won't always have to be in a meditative state when you become accustomed to doing it for a while. I can be in a conversation with someone and be doing this exercise. It's that simple and easy to master! Please don't make this harder than it is because there's no benefit for you to do that.

For the moment let's practice it in sequence until you get the hang of it. You don't even have to think about how it works or the subconscious mind versus the conscious mind. In fact, I don't want you to *think* about anything.

Just relax, enjoy the feeling of relaxation and allow yourself to use your imagination without putting fear of failure into the visualization. Just follow my instructions. I assume you're going to practice this on your lover, husband, boyfriend, "*ex*" or someone you desire. Just know and believe that it works because it does work! Okay sisters – let's go!!!

NOTE: The more you allow your heart to open using loving thoughts, forgiveness, peace and happiness the better the technique will work for you *and* for him. Emotions are the fuel so the more you have the better!

Love truly is the key to making the technique optimally effective. Open your heart and allow love to flow freely!

TRUE STORY: A reader wrote to me about her marriage and she desperately needed help. Married for over 15 years they were only living together out of necessity and there had been no intimacy for about 5 years. She was ready to leave her husband but due to her religious beliefs and heritage divorce was out of the question. She felt she was stuck for life with this man that hadn't shared her bed or her bedroom for years. After reading my book she sent me an email about her situation. She was positive I wouldn't be able to help her but she still held onto a small fragment of hope. I guided her and assured her if there was a tiny spark of love left in the relationship the technique would ignite it. Several months later she sent an email of thanks to me. Her marriage had changed so dramatically she couldn't believe it. He began to slowly change and by the time she wrote to me they were sexually active, emotionally attached, taking romantic bubble baths and happier than they'd ever been together. It was a heartwarming and touching story I'll never forget. Trust the process – it won't fail!

This is one of my favorite stories because she managed to salvage her marriage and actually create a happy environment for herself and her family. In a world where relationships are disposable, and dating is easier than ever, it's great to see lovers succeed. She wrote to me again just to say they're still doing great, still connected and she continues to use the technique to keep her hubby in line.

Chapter 5 – "Secret" Instructions

> *"No one can tell, when two people walk closely together, what unconscious communication one mind may have with another."*

You will be in a meditative or relaxed state of mind when doing the technique. So get comfortable! I usually lie on my back on the bed to meditate, and practice the technique, but if you choose to sit in a chair it's okay. Sit in a chair. The point is to be relaxed and comfortable. You can listen to music during the meditation, enjoy the quiet or listen to my special Pussy Whip guided meditation. It's your choice.

Beginners have told me they like to listen to guided meditation because it allows them the freedom to get totally relaxed and not thinking about what they need to do to relax. The whole purpose is to shift your focus from your *conscious thinking* mind to your *subconscious manifesting and connecting* mind. Now, let's go through the steps.

The **FIRST STEP** is to lie on your back on your bed (or relaxing comfortably in a chair) with your hands down by your side and your head only slightly elevated on a pillow. Get comfortable and don't cross your legs or arms. Why? You don't want to obstruct the natural energy flow from your body. Feel the bed (or chair) supporting your body perfectly before you even begin the exercise.

Take a few full, deep breaths and allow your body to relax totally as you exhale. You can inhale to the count of 4, hold the breath to the count of 7, exhale to the count of 8 if you want to relax using your breathing. If you find yourself uncomfortable in any area of your body re-position so you can feel relaxed and comfortable. Get relaxed enough so you aren't focusing on *any* discomfort in your body. The reason you don't cross anything on your body is because there are energy meridians located throughout your body and you want your energy alignment to be flowing perfectly.

You can do more research on energy points but that's what acupuncture works on when they place needles into your body. So you want your energy flowing fluidly and freely. If you're listening to my guided meditation it'll take you through all of these steps in detail so you can easily relax. Otherwise allow yourself to relax as much as *possible before beginning the visualization.*

The SECOND STEP is to get your mind and body into a state of total relaxation. If you're familiar with meditation you can put yourself in a slightly meditative state of mind. If you aren't familiar with how to meditate you can begin by focusing *only* on your breathing. Your mind can't focus on two things at once so if you focus on your breathing -- how it feels, the coolness, warmth and how it relaxes you it will calm your mind.

Basically meditation is focusing inwardly rather than on the outer world. As your thoughts focus on your breathing everything else will disappear and you will be in a light trancelike state of mind. Focus on the air going into your lungs and how that feels. Then focus on letting the air out and notice how it relaxes your body totally. When your mind wanders (and it will) just bring it back in and start focusing on your breathing, again.

Another easy and effective method to shift your mind from a conscious state to a relaxed and slightly meditative state is to repeat in your mind: *I am sleepy. I am sleepy. I am sleepy.* Or, *sleep, sleep, sleep.* This works to relax your conscious mind and engage your subconscious mind. As you're reading the book, and repeating the mantra in your mind, you may actually feel a shift from your conscious mind to your relaxed and creative subconscious mind.

The subconscious is the mind of powerful creating! This is the state of mind where you can easily manifest anything and everything you desire. *Your subconscious mind doesn't know truth from fiction.* Anything you tell it to believe it will believe. This is the mind you use during Law of Attraction techniques. It's why negative thinking is so destructive because your subconscious mind seeks out more negative things to please you. Want to change your reality? Change your thoughts!

Your subconscious mind is estimated to be 30,000 times more powerful than your conscious mind!!!

Imagine the power you have within your reach that you rarely tap into and use to your advantage. Imagine the power you have that you can direct at your mate and he has no knowledge of you using it and no chance against your *secret weapon*. He will be putty in your hands.

There's nothing you can *do, say* or *be* that will have the power of using your subconscious mind and entanglement to create what you desire in life. You can literally change your life and the direction of your relationship by just tapping in and directing your messages and feelings to your guy with intention. I keep reiterating that he'll never know it's coming from anyone else but he'll think and believe everything you're sending to him so rev up your emotions while visualizing.

THE SUBCONSCIOUS MIND WORKS WITH VISUALIZATION AND COMMANDS ONLY!

It doesn't respond to words and isn't rational. What you visualize the subconscious mind believes and attracts but it's done through emotions! You can manipulate the subconscious by believing something is true and putting the power of emotions into the belief. It's the reason when you're using the technique or using The Law of Attraction it's best if you believe the visualization.

The *sleep* mantra can literally put me into a deep sleep and I've been an insomniac my entire life. I recommend doing this only a few times until you feel your body relaxing and your awareness less focused on the outer world.

It's not necessary to worry and fret over whether you're in a subconscious state of mind because, when you're relaxed and your attention is focused inwardly, you're in a state of mind for connecting to your target. Don't bring yourself out of the proper state of mind because you fear that you're doing it *wrong*. You can't fail and you can't do it wrong! Trust me!

The **THIRD STEP** is to focus on your subject and visualize him as clearly as you can in your mind's eye. There's actually a position about an inch up from your eyebrows in the center of your forehead that's called your *third eye* or *mind's eye*. It's the area of psychic ability, visualizations and the area where you send and receive thoughts.

This area is where we do our visualization of things in the past, present or future. If I asked you to close your eyes and visualize the front door of your home, your puppy or something you experienced in your past that is the area where you'd see it.

When you're thinking of someone, or seeing a mental picture, you'll see it on this screen in most cases. To enhance your ability to *see* I suggest you tap this area lightly with your four fingertips to awaken it (at least when in the learning process). If you aren't accustomed to visualizations it'll also be a form of entrainment for your brain to know that when you tap this area it's time to use the technique.

Now feel as distinctly as possible that area in the center between your brows. Feel it like you would a powerful laser beam. Imagine the power of the area exactly like a laser beam and you'll be focusing on this area and not engaging the entire brain.

Just for a moment feel the difference. When you're thinking thoughts about something you're actually using your entire brain to do it. You can actually feel the entire inside of your head as your thoughts fill it. You'll probably be aware that both the right and left side of the brain has a balanced, full feeling.

Or, you may feel both sides of your head have an equal distribution of energy. Now focus on the third eye only and you may even begin to get a little cramp in the area between your eyebrows. This is the area I want you to use when doing this technique because it'll focus your energy and intent and be more powerful when you actually send someone a message.

Now *see* your *target* or *subject* as clearly as possible in your mind's eye or on your "*television screen*". He's standing about 40 or so feet away from you in your imagination. He's a little distance from you, as in a parking lot, but you can still see him clearly. Why a parking lot? You want him in a place where there's no one else around. Remember entanglement? The less people and distractions the better! See him all by himself, alone and with nothing around him at all including buildings.

You may not have the ability to see visual pictures in your mind's eye as well as others but it doesn't matter in this exercise. See him as clearly as you can, feel his presence or simply imagine that he's there because *he is.*

Don't worry about whether you're doing it right or not. There's no way you can do this exercise wrong. Just through your intent you'll connect to your target. Stay relaxed and don't fret over the results, whether you're doing the technique correctly, or focus on any of the other *conscious brain* type fears.

Just through your intention and focus it is working!

NOTE: If you are having doubts that this technique works it's because your conscious mind is the ever doubtful, fretting, fearful mind and it desires to keep things the same in your life. It's there to protect you and it has no interest in learning and growing. It's your fear-based mind and you have to disregard it to do this exercise.

Until you experience the power of manifesting your man back, or having him totally change, you may not believe what I'm telling you is the truth. However, every word of this book and how to manifest is not only the truth it's the absolute truth. Trust it, believe it and practice it until you become a master!

The **FOURTH STEP** is to call out to him mentally. Call out to him as if he were a block away – do it **LOUDLY**. At the same time you're mentally yelling use the laser beam I talked about and feel it connecting to him in the same area of his forehead using as much power as you can muster. This is the receiver for all communication. When you're yelling out you may even see or feel that he jumps in shock as he hears your voice. Really shout at him and get his attention. *"John! John! John!"*

Call out while remaining in a comfortable and relaxed state of mind at this time. Call to him using the power of your thoughts and see him (in your mind's eye) turn around and look at you.   See the instant recognition and imagine that he's elated to see you. He will absolutely feel the connection with you the moment you do it. In fact, wherever he is he'll receive a jolt like you sneaking up behind him and yelling in his ear.

Use your ENTANGLEMENT to your advantage!

You're beckoning to him and at the subconscious level he'll *feel* and *hear* you. It may take a few moments before you feel, see or imagine him reacting to you calling out to him. I usually call 3 times but sometimes more and sometimes less. It depends on whether I have a *sense* of being connected. You can call out as many times as necessary for you to believe you've connected to him. Just know that he will sense you, feel you, and hear you and you'll connect to him in this manner. It'll work each and every time you call out to him. I've received calls and messages immediately after (or even during) using the technique on someone and many of my readers have, too.

You may or may not have a physical sensation when you connect to him and that's perfectly fine. I'll sometimes feel absolutely nothing, occasionally I get chill bumps and sometimes I yawn as the energy connects and begins to flow. Whatever your personal reaction is don't worry about the bodily sensations and whether they happen or not.

You've called out to him and his subconscious mind hears you and responds. Remember *thoughts are things* and they are felt and acted upon immediately, especially when you use this technique. Trust it! The only thing that can stop the process is you! Think of this technique as projecting yourself to him wherever he is. Distance doesn't matter. Where he's at and who he's with doesn't matter. Nothing can stop this connection!

In actuality I believe he meets you halfway as does anyone you use this technique on. You call to them and they're summoned to appear. When that happens you'll sort of "*meet up*" in the middle if that makes sense.

The **FIFTH STEP** is to see him turn around and acknowledge you and watch him as he walks over to where you're standing. Visualize him as clearly as possible as you stand there looking at him. Some people are very visual and some are not. I happen to be someone who isn't but it doesn't matter that I don't visualize perfectly because I still get the same results and you will, too.

I'm much better at visualization now than I was when I first began. Practice has improved my visualization abilities but I got results the very first time after only a few minutes and not being a visual person. So don't worry about the visualization part because whether he's visually clear in your mind's eye or not it doesn't affect your success.

Now I want you to look into his eyes and know that you have connected spiritually, mentally and emotionally with him and you are now in complete control. Take in every detail possible while looking at him and only him. If you see yourself in the picture then you're not looking at him through your own eyes. Take note of what he's wearing, how he smells, his voice, the look in his eyes, the way his hair looks, his smile and anything else about him that you enjoy or admire.

When I use the technique emotions immediately surface for the person. I may feel love, passion, joy, sadness, sorrow, longing, anger or a thousand other emotions. Whatever they are I use them because emotions are the fuel you need for ALL manifesting. If you aren't feeling enough emotions focus on creating them in your heart area. I say this because sometimes emotions literally can be felt in every cell of your body so you don't need to manufacture them. If you are not actually feeling some type of emotion then focus on your heart area and open it up to feel. Negative emotions can sometimes shut down the heart area so when you focus on it you'll allow them to flow more freely. Emotions are the driving force behind the technique so whether it's anger, lust, love, desire, hatred or passion *all* of your emotions fuel the visualization. The more emotion about him the better so really allow yourself to let them flow.

Create and enjoy as many powerful emotions as possible during the visualization. Allow your heart area to fill with the emotions as it overflows and connects to his heart area. I feel it as connecting my solar plexus to his solar plexus. Allow the unobstructed flow of energy between your heart areas as well as between your third

ι were watching a Sci-Fi flick you'd be able to
ιrgy flowing freely between the two of you.
_.. not just imagine that energy as it goes from
you to him and back from him to you.

The **SIXTH STEP** is while mentally looking at him
I want you to hear him say what **YOU** want to hear him
say. Not what you *believe* he would actually say to you.
Just hear exactly what *you want him to say.* There's no
right or wrong here, ladies. He can tell you whatever it
is you want him to tell you. He can tell you he's a lying
piece of trash or that he'll never love anyone like he
loves you. I keep mine positive because I want to focus
on positive emotions. Your visualization is entirely
yours so visualize what you desire from him.

For instance, he may say: *"I love you. I can't live
without you. I'm sorry. I'll never love anyone the way I
love you. I'll do anything to get you back. I miss you. I
will leave my mistress. I'll change the will. I won't
require a pre-nuptial agreement. I'll take you to Belize or
Paris. I'll give you my American Express. I'll follow you
around like a puppy for the rest of your life. I'll feel sick
if I look at another woman. I'll be unable to get an
erection if I ever try to cheat. I'll be a better mate. I'll
help more around the house. I'll give you more money. I
will always be faithful."* Yes, I have made my guys say
all of the above statements and they worked. Trust me!

Whatever you want him to say is what you
visualize! I want you to listen to the words you're
putting in his mouth and feel the emotion, relief and

sheer ecstasy you feel at hearing his words. **FEEL THE EMOTION!!!** Feel the joy and happiness that he wants to do everything on *your* terms. Feel the pleasure and know that he's on his way back! Feel how happy it makes you that he'll never leave and will do everything you want him to do to keep you! Feel the joy that he'll treat you like a princess and buy you whatever your little heart desires! Allow your heart to expand and overflow with love!

You may be thinking *"words are just words"*. Nope. The thoughts you're sending, the words you're hearing him say are the precursor to the actions that will take place. He will live up to whatever you hear him say. Especially if you keep the visualizations the same for a period of time. Don't think you need to mix up the messages daily or weekly. Think of what you'd really, really like your target to do and keep it that way for a few weeks. Repetition is your friend during this process.

Remember, when you see him in your mind's eye **DON'T** visualize the two of you standing there. Imagine that this scene is happening in the moment. If you're seeing both of you then you're daydreaming. If you're seeing him standing in front of you about two feet away then you'll be focusing mainly on his head and shoulders or from his waist up.

You may even want to visualize a powerful light that goes from your third eye to his as thoughts are carried to him. Stay focused only on him during the entire visualization. If your attention strays during the process it can be caused by:

1. your meditation is too long;

2. you aren't in an alpha state; or

3. you aren't using the power of visualization and emotions.

If you are emotional about something you aren't going to have your mind wander easily. You'll be focused and enjoying the interaction!

The **SEVENTH STEP** is for you to hear yourself replying to what he has said to you. I want you to experience the feelings of happiness, relief, love, gratitude or whatever feelings his words naturally ignite within you. I want you to respond mentally to him. You may say things like *"I love you, too. I'm so happy you've come back to me. I will never let you go. You'll only be happy with me. We'll have a wonderful life together. Thank you for your generosity. Thank you for adoring me. Yes, I will marry you. We will be so happy together..."* Whatever positive statements you can make to him (and believe) will be what you'll say to him during this visualization.

I've had numerous emails from readers who say things like: "He didn't say exactly what I told him to when we got together". Does that mean that the technique failed? Or, "I wanted him to take me to lunch and in my visualization I told him that he would and he didn't".

Come on sisters! The only reason you have him say things to you is because it creates in you a feeling, an emotion that creates reality. It also places that thought in his mind because of the fuel of your emotions. What you hear needs to be something that elicits emotion in you and not something as mundane as having lunch together. Don't expect the exact words to come out of his mouth when he sees you. The thoughts and emotions are what you sent to him but if it's lost in translation that's okay.

The more emotion and the more powerful you feel the emotion, the faster and greater your manifesting will be.

After a few minutes of visualization let the feeling of peace, love, gratitude and **knowing the visualization is true** to completely wash over you. You are finished with the technique. You don't need to do anything else to ensure that it worked. It worked! I can't stress this enough. It worked!

The simple truth is that you can't fail to send him thoughts that create feelings deep in his soul and make him feel what *you* desire if you follow my instructions. The only way you can block the outcome is to worry about it, not release any expectation, have negative self-talk and sabotage your own creation. Also if you do it half-ass and go through the steps without actually the connection, using your emotions and yourself to be immersed in the visualization. Feel it, live it, experience it and love every minute of it.

When I finish the technique I release the person with love and peace and go about my day knowing that my desire will manifest. I know without question the person is as connected to me as strongly as if I were standing there holding their hand. I know I've influenced them and I'll be on their mind for a **LONG** time afterwards. It's like having great sex with someone – you just can't get them off your mind no matter how hard you try.

Realize that you've just sent a powerful message and it's impossible that he won't respond mentally or physically to your message. If he's a stubborn ass it may be a while before you hear the words directly from his mouth but he's still thinking the thoughts you sent. His actions and reactions to you will change. Pay attention to how he responds to you and don't measure your success by whether he says what you want him to say.

The minute you began using this technique it's as if you whispered into his ear or even used a megaphone to get your message across! You had his undivided attention from the moment you started the visualization. Whatever he was doing at the time he stopped and his thoughts went directly to you! Even John, who was at least playing like he was asleep, sat straight up in bed when I did it. John's energetic body is as dense and out-of-touch as his physical body.

I'm going to emphasize a few points so you understand them totally and thoroughly. You should absolutely feel regenerated, positive and confident. It's a feeling like winning the lottery or getting some sort of windfall would feel like to you.

Just the fact that you know beyond a shadow of a doubt that you connected to him, he received your message, he believes your thoughts, and actually incorporated them to be his own thoughts and you have the power to change him should make your day very special. Visualize him as if a lightbulb just went off over his head and it has a picture of you in it. He'll do just about anything right now for his Wonder Woman.

Don't get discouraged if something doesn't happen immediately.

Be patient and don't get discouraged and begin to doubt the process. Just because he hasn't picked up the phone, changed his ways or given in to you doesn't mean that his thoughts aren't driving him crazy. Remember your thoughts are now his thoughts! You're sending and receiving love from this man during your visualizations. He feels the emotions you're sending and believes them to be his own! Relax and let the process work!

Also, if he doesn't repeat the visualization word for word to you that's okay. Don't expect it! You hearing him tell you what you want to hear is not about him saying those exact words to you. *It's about igniting those feelings and desire in him.* Think about translation for a moment. If I tell you something and you tell someone else something will it be translated perfectly? The answer is no. You only care about getting him to *feel, think* and *act* a certain way and not parrot your words back to you exactly.

Why does this work so effectively, so quickly and so powerfully? Locking yourself together with the person you're contacting in this manner brings the two of you together as surely and effectively as if you were standing right in front of each other. If you think of someone, and using only The Law of Attraction, you're still inside your *own* head. Your thoughts are yours and they're not going anywhere else. It does make an imprint on your subconscious mind but it doesn't influence another person in any way whatsoever.

When you're using my technique you're outside yourself, stretching your own energetic being to another, and you'll actually be able to feel the difference with practice. There are people like Edgar Cayce who can project their awareness to other places and come back with information about things they couldn't have known. This is called astral projection or remote viewing. This technique is like that in a way because you become bigger and more powerful than just your normal, everyday self.

You're developing your mental telepathic muscle and you're also expanding your consciousness. Make yourself aware of your limited body right now, at this moment, by closing your eyes and sensing your own energetic field. It'll feel contained, smaller, tightly wrapped and close to your physical body. Now visualize a person you'd like to use the technique on to contact as you close your eyes and call them to you as you did in the exercise. You'll feel your energy body stretching, reaching and expanding.

It'll no longer be just a thought in your own mind. Your thoughts will reach out and literally touch people or things that you desire to reach. I've used this technique at auctions when I wanted to purchase something that was a hot item and everyone was in a bidding war to win. I just wrapped my energy around the inanimate object and the bidding stopped almost immediately. It's an invisible force but it's a powerful one.

When I have a friend or relative who's going through hard times I've expanded my energy body using the technique to comfort them. The first time I did it was years ago talking on the phone to a friend. I didn't tell the person I was doing anything. All of a sudden they started sobbing and I asked what was happening. They said *"I feel like you're right here with me in the room and I can feel you hugging me"*. And, that was exactly what I was doing. The connection is real and not imagined.

You can use it to influence and control your mate but you can also use the exact technique to offer comfort and support, to obtain something you desire, to expand your energy field and consciousness and to positively affect others. The wonderful thing about teaching it is the feedback from readers who've used it for such a variety of things.

One of the most common things readers say is; "*Wow, I expected it to be used only on my mate but it turned out it changed a lot of things about my life*". That's exactly the purpose of teaching the method. To expand your life and make it better and more fulfilling than it already is. You're welcome! ;-)

TRUE STORY: A friend had been married to a man for 8 months when they considered divorce. After a whirlwind 3 month romance they'd jumped into marriage too soon and they were suffering the consequences. I asked her to not make such a hasty decision without at least trying this technique. She agreed. For a couple of weeks they'd been sleeping in separate bedrooms when she began using the visualization. He began warming up to her and looking at her with more love in his eyes. He started including her when he went to do things. He began to be affectionate with her and eventually moved back into their bedroom. Within 3 weeks they were on a new, positive marital course that's lasted for 8 years now. When you use the power of your connection to strengthen a relationship it will cause it to positively shift and change. Be patient. When you think of the person during the day send them love because you're still connected to them. If you send thoughts of disappointment or anger they'll feel it. You can fix any situation if you truly want to so why not give it a try?

Chapter 6 – Your Unique Connection

"A person's mind is so powerful. We can invent, create, experience and destroy things with thoughts alone.

You are still connected! If you want to break the connection from the person just visualize the cords that go from you to him being disconnected. I visualize them like electrical plugs. Just unplug them and send them back. Why do it? Because it may cause you to feel their stress, negativity or other feelings that *aren't yours*. If you're feeling something you don't want to feel always ask yourself; *"Is this mine or someone else's?"*

Want to stay connected? During the day when you think of him, and of course you will, take yourself back to that moment in time when you were using the technique in your visualization. Feel the connection, the emotions and remember how real it felt to be so emotionally and physically close to him.

Draw on that emotion for a few seconds and then intentionally reconnect and send him a thought. It can be the same thoughts you placed in his mind earlier or it can be something totally different. It doesn't matter what the thought is for this brief moment. You are just boosting and strengthening the connection. During the actual meditation try to keep your messages the same as discussed previously.

I know you're going to think about the person *way* too often so you may as well make good use of the thoughts. Imagine pulling him to you just through your intentions and then whispering what you want to say into his ear. *"I love you"* or *"You can't stop thinking about me"* or *"You'll never be happy without me"* – or something along those lines.

What does that do? It makes you feel better for one thing. The other thing it does is keep you solidly connected and you can easily send your messages anytime you choose knowing that he's receiving them. Sometimes you may just want to take a few deep breaths and yell out to the person mentally to connect again. When you do send them feelings of love, support, forgiveness or something positive. When you see or talk to them they'll reflect back what you send in most cases.

THIS TECHNIQUE CAN'T FAIL TO MAKE HIM THINK ABOUT YOU, MISS YOU & THINK THE THOUGHTS YOU SEND!

If you find you're thinking negative thoughts, doubting the process, wallowing in self-pity, or feeling like you aren't getting confirmation – I want you to use the *"3 second rule"*. Allow yourself 3 seconds to think negative thoughts then switch them back to positive thoughts! Don't sabotage yourself with insecurity, doubt and fear. That's your conscious brain *thinking* too much! The technique is working – trust it!

I'll tell you a true story about myself and my *true love*. I was madly in love with my man for four years and during that time we had a couple of times when we broke up. I used the technique to bring him back. Once it took over three months for him to come back but he did. He's a stubborn-ass and I'm the only woman he has ever returned to.

He actually had to make-up a good reason to contact me and I guess the universe provided it to him so he sent me a text message. He had no idea that I was using the technique on him, and still doesn't even know what I write about, so it was all his idea. Or so he thinks! We were good for another year or so and then we broke up again.

The next time we broke up was when we were exactly at the four-year mark of our relationship. I loved this man very much and was devastated when we broke up. It wasn't a perfect relationship but I'm like most women and overlook the negative things and focus on the positive.

Anyway, we didn't see each other or speak for one entire *year*. He had commitment issues and I think four years is ample time to decide whether you want to settle down with someone so I stood my ground. I let him go!

I didn't chase him, call him, track him, and creep on his Facebook or social media accounts. I just let him go.

The difference is that I know the power of this technique so I used it on him. At first I used it daily and then I did the technique every few days or even less. It doesn't matter how much or how little you use it because it still works. Think of it like a cloud that contains the information you sent to the person.

The cloud doesn't go anywhere and, as long as I wanted to contact him mentally, I knew I could connect with him in an instant. I never doubted it. I *knew* he couldn't get me off of his mind. *This is where faith comes in.* I had faith because I know without a doubt that *thoughts are things* and they're real and concrete so we were entangled in a special way.

If you combine your powerful thoughts with intention, emotion and belief there's no way you can fail.

One year later he contacted me because my little nine-year-old Maltese died. He admitted to me that he'd looked for a reason for a year to come back because he thought of me and missed me every day. The minute he saw me, and I walked over to him, I knew the visualizations had not only worked but they had changed him!

He no longer had commitment issues and within weeks he proposed to me. He's now the man I deserved from the beginning but it took a year of separation for him to become that person. If I'd allowed myself to get discouraged, depressed or just given up we wouldn't be together. The time apart was good for us and I don't regret it because we both grew and we're better partners now.

Now, let me state one thing that's important for all my sisters to hear. I didn't sit by my idle phone, allow myself to lie in bed listening to sad songs, worry about him constantly or any of the other morbid things we do when we lose someone we love.

I used the technique, let any expectations go and moved forward in life.

I made new friends, went out on dates, did some extensive traveling, wrote books and even dated a celebrity. In other words, I had a life! Don't allow yourself to stay in limbo during your time apart. You'll grow from the experience and he will appreciate the changes in you. Men don't appreciate doormats or backup girls and I am certainly not that type of woman – nor should you be!

Face the fact that if things were all that great before you broke up you would most likely still be together. You both need space to grow! Allow this to be *your* time of growth, too. Don't get stuck on having only one outcome because it limits your ability to live a full, beautiful life. Be open to all possibilities!

Also, be patient during the process. I, who knows this technique works, even thought at one point *"Oh my God have I forgotten how to connect and influence?"* Yes, patience is your friend but I'm not all that patient in my personal life. I just had to trust and have faith because this technique has worked miracles in my life and I know that it never fails. I repeat – it never fails!

During our honeymoon phase of being back together I found out that I had influenced everything in his life with my secret technique. At one point, while using the technique, I visualized him saying *"Oh Lanie, where are you?"* as he paced around his home. He later told me that he would walk around his house saying that very phrase over and over again.

The songs that reminded him of me *I placed in his mind.* I would hear a song and visualize him hearing it and thinking of me. It wasn't even his type of music but he named all of the songs that made him unable to get me off of his mind. I even made a playlist of the songs!

I influenced him and created his reality with the power of my mind! No contact! No fear! No stuck in my life waiting! Every woman he went on dates with he thought *"She's not Lanie"*. And, who put that thought there? Yep, it was me!

Don't put pressure on yourself by constantly worrying about whether or not it's working. Sometimes it takes time! That shouldn't be discouraging if you're learning, growing and moving forward in your own life. Don't allow yourself to become stuck in a rut!

If you are constantly worrying about where he is, who he's with, and whether the process is working then he's controlling *YOU.* If you truly want to break the cycle, and be in control of your life, I hope you'll listen to my advice.

If you're married or in a relationship and want changes don't expect them to happen overnight but they will happen. John did exactly what he said he'd do after I used the technique but he took his sweet time doing it. Although he told me the very night I practiced the technique on him that he'd do something it took him a couple of months to follow through. Be patient. It may take time for the gears to engage and the thoughts to process and spit out results but it will happen.

You're the one who's controlling him like a puppet on a string. You need to *know* that it's working and not worry about *when* it'll materialize. The most important thing you can do to assist the process is to feel positive emotions. As in The Law of Attraction you're working with your subconscious mind and it believes what you tell it to believe without questioning it.

"Your subconscious mind doesn't know the difference between right or wrong, real or fiction, truth or lies. ALL it does is set about to make happen WHAT YOU have visualized, created and directed it to do by your thoughts and feelings."

I get questions about when to use the technique. You can practice this technique anytime you want during the day. You don't even have to lie down in order for it to work when you become proficient by practicing. Eventually, you'll be able to tap into your subconscious mind easily and with no trouble at all. As you are reading this book you can repeat *Sleep, Sleep, Sleep* and you will feel the shift in your consciousness.

You can visualize the person with your eyes open although I usually close my eyes to *see* more clearly. The point is, without dwelling on the process or person; you can tap into their subconscious mind and aura whenever you choose. Just don't forget to feel the emotion of ecstasy and gratitude knowing that he'll think the thoughts, say the words, perform the action or have the feelings you want in no time at all.

I intentionally don't do or say anything that brings harm to someone. I've grown and revenge isn't what I seek. I prefer to attract positive things in my life. Although in the case with John and his achy testicles I sometimes have a lapse in judgment. You know, I even told John exactly when the pain started, where it was and how often he felt it but he didn't believe I had anything to do with it. Oh well.

That's okay because I know the truth. My philosophy is don't mess with women who have the knowledge and power to make your nuts fall off – literally!!! I realize some of you will be non-believers and I understand. You can't know the absolute power and success of this technique until you use it for a couple of weeks. You may even write it off as a coincidence rather than give the technique credit for the changes you'll experience. I don't mind. I don't need or want kudos for teaching it to you.

Some of the readers of the book don't even try it because they're in such a negative state of mind they can't believe something like this technique could be so effective. That's okay, too. *"When the student is ready the teacher will appear."* Maybe they're just not ready, yet.

I've had more than my fair share of readers who try to rationalize their results with *it's a coincidence* or *it's just too simple to work.* Well, it does work and all you have to do is try it to find that out. If it didn't work I wouldn't be a faithful user of the technique every day of my life. I write this book, as well as my other books, to help my *sisters* not to earn the $1.50 I make off the sale of them.

I want to spread the word to all women! It's so heartwarming to get correspondence from readers who tell me about their success stories.

TRUE STORY: I received an email from a woman who had been battling her fiancé over a last-minute pre-nuptial agreement. After reading my technique and practicing it for a few weeks he voluntarily gave her exactly what she wanted and deserved. According to her he was a tightwad and he was at the point of breaking it off. Money meant more to him that she did – or so he thought. Attorneys had battled with him and he wouldn't budge. After a few weeks of her nighttime visualization he woke up one morning and told her what she visualized him saying to her. He went from a hard ass to a pussycat with just a few minutes a day of her time and focus. Pretty awesome stuff! I would absolutely love for all women to use this technique rather than sit around feeling sad, blue or out of control.

Chapter 7 – You Have the Power NOW

"Train you mind, control your thoughts, and
see the positive change in your life."

There is no limit to the number of things you can get your man to do! Whatever you can think of, and imagine in your mind, can be created through the power of this technique. Does he not want to commit to you? Is he a cheater? Is he with another woman? Is he using you for good times but also out dating other women? Is he as tight as skin on an onion and won't give you a dime? What do *you* want him to do and say to you? That's all you have to decide.

So, you know as examples when I was going through the steps of the technique we used statements like *"I love you"* or *"I can't live without you"*. You can add any other statements you want in the visualization. The most important thing is that you believe what you're visualizing. If you don't believe it then you'll block the manifestation. That's where the Law of Attraction comes into play.

I have women who have asked things like *"will you call me"* or *"come take me to lunch"*. I did use the lunch thing the very first time I tried the technique and it worked. However, I don't suggest you using that on your man. Try to create things that you'll feel passionately about. The more emotions you can create the faster and better you'll receive what you desire.

I hear from readers they believe what they're saying in the visualization but in the very next sentence they'll say *"do you think it's working"*? Well, if you're asking me that question then you don't believe it in your heart or mind. I can't visualize for you, although I have been asked to do that, but you can become a master of creating with practice.

So, let's say your man is with another woman right now. Or, he's thinking about cheating or attracted to another woman. We know these things! I can tell you what my man thinks and I also feel the energy shift when he's even remotely attracted to another woman. Men can't deny things when you use your intuitive sense and practicing the technique will cause you to become highly sensitive. Also, you are now connected in a more intimate way so you'll be even more sensitive to his thoughts. In fact, this technique makes you become *"as one"* with your mate.

If you want to come between he and another woman the best thing to do is to call him to you. Hear him tell you during the visualization *"I don't love her"*, or *"Every time I'm with her I only think of you"*, or *"Being with her makes me miss you even more"* ..... Stating specific statements helps the manifestation so I've written and published **Pussy Whip 2** which has statements that have been proven to be effective. It also includes the steps that I used when I made John's testicles feel like they were exploding and how I squeezed his heart so effectively he was headed to the hospital.

Remember, you must believe what you hear. I never think about doubt when I manifest using the visualization. Failure is not an option because I know without a doubt that he's feeling what I'm sending. I have validated it with my experiences and it's taken all doubt away totally. Get to the point where you can do the same. How can you do that? Use the technique daily and you will witness big changes in your life. It's the best way to confirm what I'm telling you.

You have the ability to tell your man what you want to hear about *ANY* subject. He'll believe it is his idea and thought. You want him to be faithful? Tell him *"you'll be unable to cheat due to guilt"*, or *"just thinking about sex with another woman will make you feel ill"*. Yes, it works! He may even say to you he could never cheat on you or he doesn't find anyone else remotely attractive.

John was my man to practice things on. He was like a brick wall and if I could get it to work on him then I could get it to work on absolutely anyone. After John and I broke up he confided that when he tried to date all he could focus on is; *"She's not Lanie and I'm not attracted to anyone else!"* Yes, you got it! That's the phrase I heard him say in my visualization. Don't feel sorry for him because trust me, he deserved it!

I didn't use the secret technique on him very often because by the time I broke up with him I was over him and the relationship. But when he would pester me I'd use it on him as a way to vent my frustration. It didn't just work when I focused on him. It worked on him for years! He couldn't move forward because the technique continued to work even though I wasn't focusing on him.

You want your guy to feel guilt? Hear him say it during your visualization. Confirm it to him when you visualize yourself responding to his statements to you. There's nothing you can't do when you use the technique. I wish you could read my emails because they would convince you without a doubt.

Women whose men have been absolutely horrible to them change their behavior. Men who've been cold and distant suddenly become lap dogs. Men who were cheating break up with their mistresses. Unaffectionate men who looked at their mates with disgust are now chasing them around the house. The men have no idea why they changed but we do!

I asked my significant other whether he thought it was evil to control a man's thoughts using mind control. Although he doesn't know about my books and technique I wanted his opinion about the subject in general. I was quite surprised by his answer.

Let me first explain why I had reservations about controlling a man's feelings if he really wasn't that into you. I'm certainly not on the man's side but due to an incident happening to me I'm sensitive about the subject of control. Years ago I had a man use this technique on me and it was against my will and my knowledge. It's the reason I make women swear not to share it with men.

I wouldn't have been attracted to this person under *any* circumstance. He was unattractive, had no personality or charm, was grossly overweight and had poor hygiene. I'm sorry if I sound arrogant but at no time in my life would I have been attracted to a man like him. However, my technique was used against me. The technique I'm teaching you was used to control me for over a year!

During that entire year I believed myself to be completely and totally in love with this guy. To the point that my friends thought I'd lost my mind. Nobody could understand what the hell I could possibly be thinking and now I can see why. But during that year I thought this man was as hot as Brad Pitt. I know it sounds crazy as hell but it's the honest to God truth. I even had dreams about him!

I know the power of the technique from the other side. I know that what the person makes you feel will absolutely feel like it's coming from you. The man you're connecting to will have no idea that his feelings aren't coming directly from his own inner desires. My experience made me not want to control someone's thoughts if I even suspected that they'd not feel that way on their own.

My fiancé' changed my mind when we discussed the subject because he said *"If the man thinks he's in love and he's happy then it doesn't matter if it's due to a mind control technique or free will"*. I guess I should have asked him about it earlier since I used the power of my mind on him for years by that time. He would have given me permission!

Men are just like us in that they want to be happy. If your visualization and the emotion of love and happiness can cause them to be in love with you and feel joy then why shouldn't it be with you and not some other woman? You can control him but you must believe it in your heart and mind. If you think he won't come back or be happy with you then he won't because of the negativity you're feeling. It's really that simple.

People say all the time *"I have no control over my life"*. Of course you have control. What you're looking at this very moment is what you've created with your thoughts. Whatever your attention is directed to will be your reality. No millionaire ever thought *"I can't be rich because I'm not talented"*. They believed just the opposite. Successful people believe they'll be successful – they don't believe they'll be failures.

Whatever you place your attention on will materialize. Think about how many times great and wonderful things have happened to you. I'm sure there are so many you can't recall but the one thing you may remember is that they happen in groups. It'll almost be like you can't do anything wrong when things are going well! Great things just keep happening to you over and over again.

The same thing happens with bad things. You may think to yourself or even voice *"Will these things never stop because it's like I have a curse on me"*. And, in a way you do. They're called your *thoughts*. Good things happen because you are resonating with them and focusing on them subconsciously and the same is true with the bad things. When your vibration is high you'll have things fall into your lap that are amazing. All good things will be attracted to you because of **YOU**.

When you're focusing on negativity and are looking for all the bad things that are sure to happen you'll get them without a doubt. You just haven't taken responsibility for them. You may find that the more you focus on the negative the worse things get. What can you do to change it? Change your focus regardless of where you're at during this point in your life and you'll change your reality.

So, visualize what you want your man to do, to be or to say. He'll never know that it's you who is influencing him and he never needs to know it. I wouldn't share it with anyone unless they understand the process and are open to new ideas. Otherwise, they may throw negativity your way if they're non-believers. Keep it to yourself so you won't have to overcome someone else's negative thoughts affecting you.

I will repeat one more time: *"There is nothing you can't get your man to do, to say or to feel"*. If you need to confirm it then you don't have the faith that it's working. Allow it to be effective by being patient during the process. If you want to contact him 10 times a day you have the ability to do it now. No need for drunk dialing or stalking. This is much more effective, anyway.

TRUE STORY: Cindy didn't want to give up on her guy but she was frustrated. I explained the secret to controlling him and she immediately used it. They had dated for several years but he absolutely refused to commit and he still wanted to hang out and drink with his guy friends. She only saw him a couple of times a week and he was growing more distant. She used the technique for about a month before she saw results but when she did they were jaw dropping. He began to see her more often, he gave up his night out with the boys, he proposed to her after several months, and they were married. She keeps me updated periodically and they've been married three years now and she has seen a complete change in him. He drinks less, loves more and has become a stay-at-home husband.

Chapter 8 – A Little "Woo-Woo" for You

> *"Thoughts become things. If you see it in your mind, you will hold it in your hand."*

I can't resist putting a little Law of Attraction information in the book because *you are always attracting.* This chapter may be *"woo-woo"* for you but try to read it and understand it because it's important in manifesting your future. You are in control of your life and your future so you should understand how you attract the things you do into your reality. The Law of Attraction works through the Universal Subconscious mind. Let's say your conscious, thinking mind has a thought or makes a statement.

> *"Your subconscious mind accepts it as fact, whether it is a fact or not"*

That thought vibrates into the universal sub-consciousness where all thoughts (positive or negative) are stored. Yes, there's a cloud which is a universal sub-consciousness that holds all thoughts *past* and *present.*

If you have a negative thought such as *"I WANT"* then all the people who want something, and their negative thoughts, will be stored there. You may not realize that "*I WANT*" is a negative statement but to want something is to recognize that you don't have the object. "*I AM*" is the statement that'll give positive results. It's a magical statement.

Let's give an example of "*I want to be rich*" because we'd all like to be wealthy. When you make a statement, or have the thought "*I WANT*", your subconscious mind vibrates as a negative thought that comes from having a lack of money.

Thoughts are stored in the universal subconsciousness of the universe and your thoughts attract *like* thoughts. All of the negative thoughts on money in the universe will resonate with your "*I WANT*" statement, such as: "*I don't have a good education*", or "*I'm never in the right place at the right time*", or "*I'm just unlucky or I will always be poor*"...

Every reason that every person believes about why they're broke will be attracted to your negative thought. Your little *nothing in your eyes* statement is magnified to infinity. Do you really understand how devastating that is to your financial well-being? I hope so, because if you grasp that fact you'll be motivated to change it.

If you send out a positive thought like "*I AM RICH*" then all the successful thoughts that are stored in the universe will be attracted to you and your thought. You'll find that you will attract money, a way to make money, an inheritance, a gift, a rich husband – the possibilities are endless.

Did you know that most wealthy people visualize their wealth increasing right before they go to sleep? That may be the reason that they also awake with creative ways to make money. They attracted the positive thoughts and successes of *all* the powerful subconscious minds and their own subconscious mind set about to make it happen.

Any statement that you make regarding something you desire to have in your life should begin with *I AM. I am rich. I am healthy. I am loved. I am desirable. I am beautiful. I am lucky. I am skinny.* You get the idea. Never, ever have a thought that begins with *I WANT.* The affirmations I create for meditations begin with "*I AM*". Two of the most powerful words in the dictionary.

Your subconscious mind will create what you believe. If you believe you want something that you don't already have you will doom yourself to failure. Wanting something will create more wanting.

Desire is different, however. We all desire things and it's the driving force in life. Desire things with the knowledge that you'll have what you desire. If I see something I don't currently have I don't look at it and want it. I look at it and think to myself "*I desire that and it is mine*" and then I feel the emotions of having and enjoying the thing I desire. To attempt to change your circumstances before you change your visual picture of it is to struggle against the very nature of things. There can be no outer change until there is first an imagination and belief change.

The easiest, fastest and most effective way to manifest is to let your passion and desire guide you. What you're passionate about is what you should have in your life. It doesn't matter if it's a person, a job, a fortune, a puppy, a home, a car or a vacation. Follow your passion because it ignites your ability to attract it without any effort at all. Your passion and excitement is already setting in motion the wheels of manifesting.

"Live your life in gratitude of your good fortune."

When you're doing your visualization don't visualize as if it's a future event. Visualize it as if you're living it right now, today and in this moment. If you visualize something in the future you're just doing a little mindless daydreaming. If you visualize something in the past you are reminiscing. If you visualize something in the *now* you are creating!

Recognize that your subconscious mind will create your reality as it does every day of your life. Whether you realize it or not you're creating your reality minute-by-minute and day-by-day. You've just been doing it passively. Now you'll get involved in doing conscious creation and it'll create the life you'd like to have and not the life you've created by default.

You may not have realized that you are the creator of your circumstances. You may not have been awakened to the fact that you create your own reality. Whatever dreams you want fulfilled can be lived by you and created by you! You have the power to create! Enjoy it to the fullest!

TRUE STORY: My friend Dawn wanted a home with a pool, a man who adored her and the ability to travel. She was married to a cheapskate who refused to give her the life she deserved even though he could have afforded to do so and he kept her on a tight budget. He ended up divorcing her and leaving her with two small girls at home. As a stay-at-home mother she was unsure what she could do to earn a living much less realize her dreams. She met a man who gave her everything she dreamed of and more within about 6 months so she never had to support herself or her children. They live in a beautiful 5,000 square foot home with a resort style pool, have a second home in Colorado which she had always dreamed of having and they travel extensively. Did I mention he treats her children as if they were his own?

Chapter 9 – Success Tips

"Do not give up! The beginning is always the hardest."

I receive many questions that I answer personally but I also created a forum to answer questions due to the sheer volume I receive daily. I think women want to make using the technique harder than it really needs to be. Maybe we're accustomed to having to fight for everything we receive in life so if it's too easy it seems that it shouldn't work.

Maybe it's that we don't believe we're entitled to have the power in a relationship. Whatever the reason doesn't matter. This technique has been used by me and thousands of others to create lives that are powerful, amazing and unbelievable.

I hope my *sisters* don't mind that I've shared things with you while leaving out their identity. The actress that I wrote about was on a primetime series. Of course, she wrote to me about her man but what happened to her because of her meditation, visualization and change of belief was that the man became less important as time went on.

She created a life that is enviable to others because once you know that you have the ability and power to manifest you realize that it can spill over into every aspect of your life. She is now an "A" list actor who has the right of first refusal without auditioning for roles. She credits the power of visualization and using my *secret technique* for her success.

Yes, she did get the guy back and to my knowledge they're still together. I write about the fact that if it is a full-time job to keep the man he may not be worth it. If he's in love with you it will magnify the love. If not, he'll come back but may lose interest if you don't continually control him with your thoughts.

Another reader shared that she hadn't been intimate and loving with her husband for a long, long time. They lived their lives as strangers in the same house. She thought it was time for a divorce but she decided to try the secret technique as a last-ditch effort. Within a couple of weeks his attitude changed and he was responding positively to her.

Within a couple of months they were like newlyweds! They'd gone for a period of years without intimacy and they were bathing together, enjoying vacations and their relationship and interaction totally changed. From a marriage of cultural convenience to a passionate, loving relationship in a short amount of time. The only thing she did differently was use the technique and she was elated! She saved her marriage but more importantly she *changed* her marriage. Anything is possible when you use the technique.

So many of my readers have stated that *all* of their past loves, new love interests and most men became attracted to them or came back into their lives I can't even estimate the number. You are broadcasting on a different frequency the moment you begin the visualization and you're expanding your own consciousness. That's attractive and desirable to both sexes.

Using this technique will make you more attractive to all men and old loves will come back around.

Some old loves that have been gone for 10 or more years will come knocking at your door. First of all, when you meditate you resonate with earth's energy and, when you resonate at that energy, you are resonating with the power of the earth. I use music on my guided meditations that utilize the Schmann's Resonance which is thought to cause a positive effect on thoughts, emotions and behavior.

As you continue to practice meditation your belief in the process will grow stronger and you'll become more healthy, vibrant, rejuvenated and in control of manifesting. When you think of something it'll almost magically appear. It's called synchronicity. When I ask a question the answer will show up without me having to search for it.

Someone or something will bring the answer to me and usually it's the least expected manner. I don't question or demand anything of the universe because *I KNOW* that *I AM* but a small piece of a very large puzzle. But I am an important piece. So are you!

Whether you know it or not you're a special and unique person and whatever you ask for, whatever you desire is noted and a process is begun to deliver it to you. One of the greatest feelings to have that will expedite the blessings is *IT IS DONE* or *ISN'T IT WONDERFUL.* The emotions behind both statements create a peaceful feeling, a feeling of the wish being fulfilled that ignites the universe to deliver it to you. Faith and trust are critical if you want to manifest.

During my visualization I focus on sending messages with my heart chakra because I know the power of the heart area. In fact, it's claimed that the heart mind is more powerful than the mind between your ears. It's a powerful manifesting space to concentrate on and opening your heart area is also beneficial to your health, your spirit and your connection to the powerful universe.

Whenever possible I use the heart area to send loving thoughts to those I love. I usually receive a message or a phone call because the feelings I send are felt by the person I'm thinking about. Miracles will begin to happen in your life if you allow them to.

When you're in touch with the universe you may be surprised at things that happen. I once was driving down the highway in the left lane and clearly got the message that I was going to be hit by an oncoming car.

I immediately slammed on my brakes and moved over right before the oncoming car crossed the double yellow line.

I listen to the universe and I have total faith and trust in it! I hope you learn that you are always attracting things to you that you're open to receiving. Keep the lines of communication open and don't close your mind to the world you cannot see.

It's estimated that we experience less than 1% of what's really in the world to see, feel and experience. I don't know if that's true but I would estimate that it's even less than 1%. We can't possibly think this is all there is to life with our limited bodies, mental capacity and chatterbox minds. Be open to experience more and you will experience amazing things!

When you want to connect without going into a full meditation you can do so easily. If you're talking to someone, and you want to influence them, just visualize your mind reaching out to theirs for a little mental telepathy. It's a quick way to positively influence someone you're meeting for the first time. Shake their hand, look into their eyes, and say to them mentally; *"You're going to really, really like me."* You'll almost hear their sighs as they relax when they receive your message.

Remember, the minute you look at someone you are entangled with them at a quantum physics level. The minute you think of someone you're connected to them at the same level. Distance and time don't matter in this state. Rather than feel your thought in your own mind *see* it reach out to *touch* the other person. Your connection will eventually be strong enough you can actually feel their environment, know their mood and be able to influence them *instantly*.

> **TRUE STORY**: A client of mine began using the technique and it enhanced her own psychic ability so much that she began her own healing and telepathic guidance classes. When you expand your consciousness you'll notice more synchronicities in your life and you'll be more aware on a deeper level. She didn't know she was a natural born healer until she began working on her husband to get him to treat her better. He improved but so did everything else in her life. She now has a flourishing business, a wonderful marriage and is happier and more fulfilled than she's ever been. Open your mind to ALL possibilities!

Chapter 10 – Questions & Answers

"Imagination is everything. It is the preview of life's coming attractions."

I'll share the most common questions with you. I hope it helps. Please join my forum for additional insight and personal responses from me and other forum members. It's a forum designed to empower women and it's a wonderful, safe place to receive encouragement from *sisters*.

Q: Can I do the technique wrong?

A: No, it's impossible to do it wrong. There's no way that a directed thought does not hit the *target*. It is impossible! He will feel you, sense you, feel your emotions and think the thoughts you place in his head when you use this technique.

Q: How do I know is my subconscious mind is engaged?

A: You don't have a switch that you can turn on and off but when you are in a relaxed state of mind, and not actively thinking, you are in a good state of mind to connect and influence. If you are lying (or sitting) there and thinking about making a sandwich then you aren't in the right frame of mind. Focus your mind *inward* and you are moving into your subconscious state of mind. *Focusing on your breathing is enough to gently shift your consciousness.*

Q: What if I can't *see* him?

A: Close your eyes right now and *see* your bedroom. That's as much detail as you need to *see* to make the technique work. It isn't a clear picture of your room but you can visualize the way it looks, what's in it and how it *feels*. That's as much as you need to do to get in touch and connect with your target. You'll become better and better at visualizing as you go along. Don't worry about it because you'll block the connection.

Q: Can I break up a romance?

A: Your thoughts can strengthen or lessen feelings between two people because you're interfering with the wavelength between the two people you're trying to break up. Let's say your *ex* has a new girlfriend. You can visualize the two of them not having fun together, having a disconnection, being emotionally distant, having arguments or just growing apart. The power of your mind (because you can now intentionally send messages) is far greater than anyone you know. So yes, you can come between two people. It's up to you whether you want to or not. I also have meditations on my website created specifically for keeping your man faithful.

Q: Why does it take longer to manifest some things and others happen immediately?

A: The more you *want* something the further it gets from you! If you are really *wanting* a mate in your life then you're pushing him further away from you. The worry about whether someone's going to come back or not means that you doubt the process. Don't doubt it! Doubts are your enemy!

Live your life as if the person's going to be walking up to your door at any moment and see what happens. Things that you may not care much about may manifest faster because you *let go of expectations* and don't worry about the outcome. That's the best possible way to manifest what you desire.

Also, I'll reiterate if you want to manifest faster, and you want the manifestations to be in your highest good, use your heart to manifest. Allow love to flow freely to your mate and they'll feel the love and respond to it. Manifesting from a total ego-oriented space, where all you care about is you, is not as productive or fulfilling. When love flows miracles happen!

Q: Can I ask for signs that the universe is listening?

A: Sure, if you aren't doing it because you doubt the process. I ask for signs sometimes but just to know that I'm connected. I was at a market one day and before I checked out I asked the universe to tell me something that I could verify so I would know if I was connected to universal energy. I *heard* a message that the guy checking out my items had 2 sisters and 1 brother. I got up to him and asked if there were 4 children in his family. "*Yes*" he replied. I asked if he had 2 sisters and 1 brother. He looked shocked but answered, "*Yes, do I know you?*" If it's just to keep in touch I think it's okay to asked for signs from universal intelligence.

Q: How do I know when to give up if I want someone back?

A: Well, it took me a year before my man returned but during that time I didn't worry about it. If it was in my highest good I knew he'd come back. In the meantime, I moved on and had a great life. No sitting around or crying in my pillow.

You can give up and move on knowing that he still gets your messages through your mind power, intention and your entanglement connection but he has the free will to react to them or not. In other words, don't spend your life stuck in the past because *time is the one thing that can't be replaced.* Move forward and know that you can contact him at any time mentally. Save the text messages and creeping on him because they don't work!

Q: Can he block my mental messages?

A: No. The interaction and message is received instantly although it may take a little bit of time to process. I visualize my messages as a cloud that's waiting there for an opening before descending on the person. That may sound ominous but it's not intended to be. It's just that thoughts are energy and they don't dissipate or disappear. The target (when using the technique) can't escape the thoughts you're sending. They'll reach them instantly but I also like to visualize them hanging around for a long time. Do I know that happens? Yes. I've gotten feedback from others that they'll continue to think the thoughts I sent for *days*!

Q: Some days I feel connected and positive and other days not so much is there anything I can do?

A: Yes, you can feel positive ALL the time. If you know that a check is in the mail do you feel happy or sad about it? View contact with your target as a check in the mail and know that he's connected to you, feeling you, missing you and receiving your messages.

If you can't focus, or don't feel up to contacting him with emotion, don't waste your time doing the technique. Take a day off. Sometimes we just don't care enough or desire them enough to do it. I took plenty of days or even weeks off during my year hiatus with my significant other. It's okay because he still thought about me many times during the day!

Q: Will I absolutely, positively and totally be successful using your technique?

A: Well, if you follow my instructions you'll connect to the person you desire, make him (or her for the men cheating and reading the book) feel the emotions you are sending and making them miss you, think of you and desire you. And, they believe it's all coming from within themselves. Would you call that a success? I would say so!

It's like reading a diet book as an example. If you read, understand and follow the suggestions then you'll be successful on your quest to lose weight. If you read the information and set it on the shelf without following the diet you won't lose an ounce of weight. You have to do what the book suggests. If you do your life will change in numerous ways! In the most positive, exciting and empowering ways! I know that without a doubt!

Q: What happens if I envision my man coming back to me and he visualizes himself with another woman?

A: That's a tough one because I used to believe it would be the one who has the most powerful visualization and belief system. That is if you were only dealing with the Law of Attraction. This is much more powerful than that. If you are weak-minded and not convinced, and he's hell bent determined, then it would be my guess that he'll manifest his reality. However, please asked yourself if you really want someone with you if they want someone else. My answer would be *no* but yours may be different.

If you practice sending positive, loving thoughts you'll benefit because it'll heal your heart and allow you to move forward. He'll feel the love, and not the distrust or resentment, so the chances of him returning are magnified. It's manifesting in each of your highest good that I recommend.

Q: Why do I visualize him and hear him but it is in my voice?

A: It'll be in *your* voice and not his. It's your thought. Don't worry about it because it doesn't matter at all. Zero, zip, zilch.

Ladies, I hope you use the suggestions in the book, follow the process and enjoy the results! Understand that it's a process and it should be an enjoyable one. You should feel absolutely wonderful after you do the technique! It should be something you look forward to doing daily and not feel like a chore that you need to get out of the way.

TRUE STORY: Rebecca was in a relationship with her guy for 6 months before he ghosted her and she wanted him back. She used the secret technique on him and he returned only to leave again. He was flaky but she loved him. He'd come back for a period of time and then leave again. Turned out he was dating another woman at the same time. Rebecca was devastated but determined. She used my "Stop Your Man From Cheating" meditations to surround her guy with HER energy and within a couple of months the other girl was gone. Rebecca never told him how she'd used her own energetic body to surround him and repel ALL women. They eventually moved in together and they've now set a wedding date. Nothing's impossible when you know how to use specific techniques to get your man, keep him and prevent outside interference. ☺

Pussy Whip meditation available ONLY at:
http://laniestevensauthor.com

Made in the USA
Monee, IL
28 October 2020